Defusing the Angry Patron:

A How-To-Do-It Manual for Librarians®

Second Edition

Rhea Joyce Rubin

HOW-TO-DO-IT MANUALS®

NUMBER 177

Neal-Schuman Publishers, Inc.

New York   London

Published by Neal-Schuman Publishers, Inc.
100 William St., Suite 2004
New York, NY 10038

Printed and bound in the United States of America.

The paper used in this publication meets the minimum requirements of American National Standard for Information Sciences—Permanence of Paper for Printed Library Materials, ANSI Z39.48-1992.

Library of Congress Cataloging-in-Publication Data

ISBN 978-1-55570-731-6

CIP Pending

Contents

List of Figures

Preface

Violent crime at a library always grabs the headlines, but fortunately most libraries never deal with shootings, assault and battery, or sex crimes. The most frequent security issue is theft of library materials. And the most common problem situation in libraries involves an angry patron.

The term *problem patron* is usually an inaccurate descriptor. Except in rare, extreme circumstances, the patron alone is not the problem. Instead, the interchange between patron and staff is (or becomes) a problem. The overwhelming majority of these difficult exchanges involve anger, rather than other issues such as violence.

As the Fairfax County (VA) Public Library states in its *Problem Behavior Manual*:

> It's important for staff to understand that customers will be angry, rude or careless from time to time. . . . We must understand that these are not true problem behaviors, and that customers do have a right to be angry and to express unhappiness with our facility and our services. . . . Every customer is entitled to their own style of using the public library, as long as it doesn't interfere with others.

A decade ago the number one cause of stress and anger in patrons—and library staff—was other library users who refused to vacate computer workstations when their allotted time was up. That era was before time-out software was invented; such software took the burden of timekeeping away from library staff since it controls the length of each user's session. The number two cause of anger was patrons waiting in line for a computer. Now most libraries use reservations software for people to prearrange their computer time (on at least some of the computers), so there are fewer lines.

As I write this, the world is in dire financial straits and we have the highest unemployment rate in America in over 50 years. Library use is at an all-time high. And people are fighting over computers again (or maybe still). Libraries report that issues around using the computer are still the number one problem causing patrons (and staff) stress and anger. The stress points include availability of computers, technical problems with them, and privacy concerns.

According to my informal survey of public and academic libraries in ten states, three issues share the number two ranking of most commonly reported stress points. These are circulation policies (including fines and claimed returns), handling people with mental health problems and/or homeless people (especially in urban libraries), and dissatisfaction with services (everywhere). The latter includes patrons who turn belligerent when they are told that the library cannot fill a request (for materials or services).

The fact that angry patrons present serious dilemmas for library staff has not changed either. Anger is contagious, so talking with (and listening to) an angry person can cause staff to feel angry, frustrated, victimized, and/or helpless. This secondhand anger is not new either.

Who Should Read This Book?

This book is for all library staff members who are:

- sick and tired of being yelled at by patrons;
- unsure what to do when someone looks angry;
- ready to get on with their jobs;
- frightened by the unexpected high emotion over a simple library transaction;
- angry themselves because they feel dumped on by the public; and
- frustrated by their own behavior under pressure.

We do not need to feel powerless in the face of anger. We can take control of the situation and feel better about ourselves while, at the same time, calming the patron, solving the presenting problem, and moving on to assist the next patron.

This book is not primarily about behavior that threatens public safety or interferes with others' use of the library's services, although some of these situations are addressed. In most cases, such behavior is illegal and must be settled with the assistance of the police. This book *is* about the everyday occurrence we all dread: the patron who is upset about a library policy or procedure and vents his or her considerable anger on staff.

Direct and practical, *Defusing the Angry Patron* is a workbook, not a textbook. It seeks to:

- put anger into context;
- use real library situations;
- offer various techniques, so you can find the one that's comfortable for you;
- present scripts as examples from which you can create your own;
- give exercises so you can practice your new skills;
- suggest methods to release your own stress and anger; and
- provide tools to use on the job.

How Is This Book Organized?

Chapter 1, "A Primer on Anger," summarizes anger research that points to methods for dealing with this difficult emotion. The chapter includes an exercise designed to help you consider your own actions when you are angry and your reactions when confronted with an angry person. To make the most of what you read, take the time to do this exercise and the others that appear throughout the book.

Chapter 2, "Preventive Measures," suggests actions which can minimize the number of angry patrons you see. Some of these are things you as an individual can do, such as welcoming patrons as they arrive; others are for the library as an institution to do, such as signage. Included is a discussion of the expectations and attitudes of patrons and of staff.

The heart of the manual is Chapter 3, "How to Do It." This chapter presents 25 basic strategies for defusing anger in a patron or any other human being. Exercises are given so you can practice these strategies to see which ones fit you best. Some will feel more natural and will work better for you than others. Try them out!

Perhaps the most important technique for calming an upset person is to listen carefully. Thus, Chapter 4 is "Effective Listening Skills." As in the rest of the book, I encourage you to create your own responses rather than to memorize these.

Chapter 5, "Beyond the Basics," addresses difficult situations which are different from, yet similar to, dealing with anger. Complaints, accusations, and unacceptable behaviors are discussed. Completely new in this edition, Chapter 6, "The Digital Landscape," addresses the unique issues of handling anger on library webpages, blogs, and more.

The final two chapters focus on you rather than the patron. Chapter 7, "Coping with Your Own Anger," suggests ways of letting go of the stress and emotion we so often pick up from people who are angry. Chapter 8, "Help Is at Hand," offers practical tools for you to use when coping with angry patrons.

At the end of each chapter is a "Quick Review." You can use this to review what you have read or to share major points with a coworker or friend. In Chapter 8, the Quick Reference Guides section provides "cheat sheets" (see Figure 8.1) which summarize the key techniques in the book; use these as cards to keep with you or post them on your desk or computer. A bibliography and index complete the book.

Where Did This Book Originate?

I first started working with angry patrons as a jail librarian in the 1970s. My angry patrons included both inmates and correctional officers who were quick to anger and difficult to reason with. Public libraries in the area asked me to help their staffs learn techniques for coping with animosity, and so began 37 years of interest in this topic.

Besides my own experiences, *Defusing the Angry Patron* reflects the comments and experiences of 10,000 public and college librarians and paraprofessionals who have attended my workshops on the topic, as well as dozens of reference librarians, circulation staff, and other public and academic library workers in ten states who responded to a short, informal survey I conducted in 2009.

What's New in This Edition?

What has changed in the 11-year gap between the first edition of this book and this second edition?

Incidents with angry patrons have increased significantly, according to anecdotal evidence; firm statistics are difficult to find. For example, on May 31, 2010, *Library Hotline* reported that the director of the Kansas City (MO) Public Library "acknowledged to the local press . . . jumps in reported incidents of more than 50% from 2008 to 2009 . . . ." In June 2010, the director of the Central Library and the deputy executive director for Branch and Outreach Services explained to me in a telephone conversation that the newspaper reporter quoted by *Library Hotline* had not understood the difference between "behaviors" and "incidents" so her report was not accurate. They clarified that any one reported incident can be categorized in more than one way, and the staff members' perceptions of any one incident may vary, so the rise in reported behaviors may not reflect such a large actual increase in incidents. Yet e-mails I exchanged and phone interviews I conducted with librarians across the country that same month confirmed that the rate of encounters with angry patrons has greatly accelerated recently, although it has not been documented. The bad economy, the growing presence of homeless people at the library, and the unusually large demand for library services were usually cited as the reasons.

Customer service workers in the for-profit sector have also seen an increase in the number of angry customers, according to the *Wall Street Journal*. They "face more frequent personal attacks than people in most other occupations, with little or no opportunity to respond . . . as a group, customer service people are more prone to illness, absenteeism, stress-related disability claims, and family leave requests . . ." (Shellanberger, 2004).

Meanwhile, patrons' expectations have risen dramatically during the past decade. Options have proliferated in terms of formats and media, as well as expedited delivery methods. Self-service and 24/7 services via websites were new expectations—which most libraries did not meet— ten years ago. Now those advances are commonplace, and users have developed even higher expectations, especially in terms of speed. After all, young adults shun e-mail and phone calls for instant messaging and texting, and e-book readers can download entire books in under a minute. Unrealistic expectations yield frustrated users.

In 2000, there was much talk about the narcissistic "Me Generation," characterized by selfish, discontented, and entitled attitudes. In 2009, one spin doctor opined,

During the past five years, a new attitude and a segment of American society has emerged—the *"Fed-Ups"*—along with a brand-new lexicon. In the past, the discontented constituted merely a slice of the population. Today, the Fed-Ups are nearing a majority of the population. In the past, the unifying emotion was anxiety [a mixture of fear and hope]. Today, it is frustration....

And frustration is entry-level anger.

Libraries have changed in the past decade, too. In relation to angry patrons, I note five key changes.

1. **Behavior Policies and Procedures**. Most libraries are crafting their behavior policies more carefully, taking into account various lawsuits on the topic. For example, courts have ruled that a library is a limited designated public forum, with the right to enforce reasonable rules of conduct in keeping with its mission, as long as it also protects the rights of the public to use it. Other court decisions have forced libraries to write policies focused narrowly on specific behaviors without violating patrons' First Amendment, due process, and other rights. A related recent development is that more libraries are creating procedures to enforce those behavior policies.

2. **Penalties**. Many libraries are taking a tougher stance with people whose anger blows out of control ("like lit fuses") to keep staff (and other patrons) from being intimidated. It used to be that libraries did not ask patrons to leave unless their behavior was blatantly illegal or dangerous. Now many libraries are being proactive and enforcing stiffer penalties more readily. Patrons who are behaving in ways proscribed in the policies (e.g., disrupting the everyday operations of the library) are asked to stop, with the warning that if they do not comply they will be asked to leave. This tougher position may be a reaction to the current overcrowding in many libraries; or it may be the result of the success of the "broken window" theory of intervention. Criminologist James Q. Wilson coined the term when research found that a broken window which is not fixed immediately is a predictor of a neighborhood's decline. It seems that one broken window leads to more broken windows, so if each broken window (or misbehavior) is taken care of immediately, a community will feel that social order prevails.

3. **Security Staff**. Many more public libraries, as well as academic and special libraries, employ private security guards, usually through contracting with a security firm to provide and supervise the personnel. A 2008 study of Ohio's public libraries found that 25 percent have security officers, either in house or contractual, which is a higher percentage than in the past. Meanwhile, a few innovative libraries have agreements with the local police departments or social service agencies to work in the library, assisting both library patrons and staff with difficult situations.

These people are paid by the library but are hired and supervised by their respective departments.

4. **Virtual Reference Service (VRS) and other remote services**. In addition to traditional face-to-face (FtF) reference, most libraries now commonly offer virtual reference service via e-mail, instant message (IM), text, or chat. Some practitioners feel that the anonymous and faceless nature of VRS frees patrons of social constraints so that they express anger more easily, but research has found that only 4 percent of remote users were angry or rude during VRS. The basic interpersonal skills which librarians use in FtF or telephone reference serve them well in VRS too.

5. **Web 2.0 and Social Media**. The new interactive web allows easy, instant interactions between users and libraries as well as among users. Many libraries have jumped into the digital age by creating their own blogs and by creating a presence on Facebook, Twitter, and other social network sites. They are harnessing the power of social media to publicize library programs and services. Word-of-mouth publicity becomes viral marketing because comments (and responses) spread so quickly on the web. The downside is that complaints, angry comments, and misinformation also spread quickly. One dissatisfied user can broadcast his or her complaints to millions of people worldwide with a few clicks on a computer keyboard. Libraries are just beginning to comprehend the many and huge impacts of Web 2.0 and social media.

The strategies and exercises in the pages that follow are designed to give all library workers the tools they need to prevent angry confrontations and to quickly defuse those that do arise. My hope is they will make libraries a safer and better environment for both users and workers.

Acknowledgments

The first edition of *Defusing the Angry Patron* relied heavily on stories and tips from more than 10,000 librarians and paraprofessionals who had participated in my workshops across the United States since 1980. While this revised edition retains many of those stories, it is enriched by newer ones that I heard in workshops or that were sent to me in response to an informal survey that was part of my research this year. I am grateful to each and every person who shared their experiences and expertise.

My hat's off to Jane Berliss-Vincent for teaching me Dragon Naturally-Speaking 10, a speech recognition program. This software by Nuance enabled me to avoid sitting; I dictated into a Bluetooth headset and watched my words (more or less accurately) appear on my computer monitor. Thanks, too, to Paula Murphy for her excellent bibliographic research, to Cailin Yeager for super-fast proofreading, and to Barbara Cohen for her last-minute rescue.

I continue to appreciate Kathleen Weibel and Pat Schuman's interest in my work. Without their intervention, way back in the early 1970s, I would not have published my first book. Thanks to Mary Kay Chelton, who nominated that book for the Shaw Award for Library Literature. Without that, I may not have written another word.

I am most grateful, always, to my husband, Larry, and daughter, Hannah, who have contributed in countless ways to each of the 13 books I have written during the past 35 wonderful years.

A Primer on Anger

What Is Anger?

Frustrated, upset, angry, or furious. One of these adjectives usually describes the patron in a problem situation in the library. A regular patron refuses to pay a fine, a pillar of the community throws a book when told that it cannot be renewed, a student shouts obscenities about the policy on reference materials, or a paragon of respectability refuses to let anyone else use an Internet terminal. What is going on? Their behavior tells us that they are angry. But what *is* anger?

A Protective Mechanism

People become angry to protect themselves when they are under a lot of stress. Sociologists and psychologists theorize that daily life has become so stressful that free-floating frustration is common. Meanwhile, our fast-paced society has become accustomed to instant gratification—one-hour cleaners, half-hour film developing, and ATMs are old news in an age where texting and instant messaging are prevalent. The combination of daily stress and high expectations leads to frustration when anything moves slowly or goes wrong. Then a person focuses all of his or her pent-up ire on the immediate cause. So, waiting in line at the reference desk may produce an angry outburst disproportionate to the situation.

Although it's small consolation when you are the target of anger, *all* service positions are dealing with this society-wide problem. Studies of the ten most stressful professions always list customer service representative in the top ten, along with police officer, air traffic controller, and firefighter. Public expression of anger is so commonplace that it has spawned a new vocabulary, including the terms *road rage* (one driver screaming at another) and *aisle rage* (a passenger screaming at the bus driver).

The two most common ways to protect oneself in response to stress and conflict are *avoidance* and *dominance*. These techniques are also known as the fight-or-flight response, a biological process that humans share with animals. In order to avoid conflict, or to end a confrontation

Anger is a brief lunacy.
                                    —Horace

There was never an angry man that thought his anger unjust.
                    —Saint Francis de Sales

quickly, most people flee the situation (avoidance) or fight to win (dominance). An angry person avoiding a situation may actually leave or may withdraw into silence; this flight response is passive. An angry person who wants to dominate may yell or show aggressive physical behavior, such as pounding the desk; this fight style is aggressive. Neither the submissive nor the dominant person is willing to look for a mutual solution. What is really needed is for one person to adopt a third response: problem solving. (This will be discussed more fully under Strategy 22: Be Assertive in Chapter 3.)

One way to defuse anger is to lower the stress level. For example, people at a picnic do not anger as easily as the same people would in the employment application line. For the library this means that the more comfortable and pleasant we make the general atmosphere, the less likely we will witness uncontrolled anger. Have you noticed that the loan area in your bank has comfortable seating and complimentary coffee and tea? Libraries can adapt that idea by providing chairs for patrons who are waiting in line. Or take an idea from bakeries by providing take-a-number machines so that patrons can pull a number and then browse other areas of the library while waiting their turn. Similarly, if we assist patrons in reducing stress by decreasing their defensiveness, we can minimize the chance of anger. For example, if staff explains upfront to a new patron that *all* new cardholders are limited in the number of books they may check out, the patron may not take it personally and become angry.

A Secondary Emotion

Anger is often a mask over another emotion; that is, it is the visible emotion (called the secondary emotion) which develops in response to another (the primary) feeling. This is significant to us, because one way to handle anger is to discover and deal with the primary emotion. Often the primary feeling is a loss of self-esteem, so we usually can dissipate the anger by increasing self-esteem, trust, or pride.

You do not need to be a psychiatrist or social worker to do this. You can increase someone's self-esteem simply by treating patrons courteously. It is a truism that everyone deserves respect; more important is the fact that every individual *feels* that she or he *deserves* respect. And when she or he doesn't get it, anger may surface. For example, if a professor is irritated while using the college library, a staff member can help the situation by addressing the patron as "doctor" or another appropriate honorific. By doing this, the staff person demonstrates respect, boosting the professor's self-esteem and thereby lessening the chance of anger.

Other common emotions masked by anger are embarrassment and fear. Let's look at some examples. A regular patron may be embarrassed when told she has an overdue fine or may feel that the library is not showing her due respect. By calling the patron by name and acknowledging her status as a frequent patron, the circulation staff member may be able to defuse any anger. Or the patron may be embarrassed in front of you and family members or friends accompanying him about not having enough money on hand; by explaining that he can pay the fine next time, the staff person can eliminate that discomfort. Another possibility is that the patron is afraid, perhaps of losing her borrowing privileges. With young patrons, especially, there can be a real fear that parents will get angry. By allowing the person to still check out some materials, the staff person can defuse both of these situations.

Anger can also mask feelings of guilt. Ironically, some people feel guilty for feeling angry and then feel resentful of the object of the anger (i.e., you) for making them feel guilty. A patron can sometimes be calmed just by acknowledging the difficult situation, because that awareness alleviates the sense of guilt. For example, if there is a long, slow line to reach the circulation desk, a staff member can help an angry patron calm down by immediately suggesting that waiting in line is frustrating. This is also true when trying to use a broken printer or a malfunctioning copier.

You can tell that anger is a secondary emotion by how quickly it disappears and is replaced by another feeling, especially when new information is introduced. For example, a high school student may be angry to find someone else using his carrel; the person feels ownership of that desk—overlooking the square—where he studies every day and feels that he "deserves" that window seat. When shown that a new row of carrels has been installed closer to the window, the patron no longer cares about his customary desk because he now has a better view (which he "deserves").

> Anger is a response to a perceived misdeed.... Anger involves an attribution of blame.
>
> —W. Doyle Gentry

EXERCISE

Self-Test

I. Think about the last time a patron—or anyone else—expressed anger at you.

1. Who was the person?

2. How did you know this person was angry at you?

3. What did she or he say to you?

4. What did she or he do?

5. How did you respond? Check all that apply:

____ Yelled back	____ Called police prematurely	____ Minimized the situation
____ Gave an ultimatum	____ Felt guilty	____ Took it personally
____ Walked away	____ Magnified the situation	____ Grew silent
____ Cried	____ Used sarcasm	____ Other—please explain:

(Cont'd.)

EXERCISE (Continued)

6. How did you feel during the interaction? Check all that apply:

____ Angry	____ Frustrated	____ Guilty
____ Frightened	____ Pressured	____ Powerful
____ Nervous	____ Defensive	____ Powerless
____ "Why me?"	____ Misunderstood	____ Other—please explain:

7. How did you feel afterward? Check all that apply:

____ Angry	____ Vengeful	____ Sorry
____ Exhausted	____ Nauseated	____ Embarrassed
____ Other—please explain:		

8. Other memories/comments:

II. Let's look at the flip side of the situation. Remember a recent time when you expressed anger at a friend, coworker, or relative.

1. Who was the person?

2. What did you say?

3. What did you do during the interaction? Check all that apply:

____ Screamed	____ Made demands	____ Name-called
____ Cried	____ Used sarcasm	____ Mind-read
____ Exaggerated	____ Pounded or threw something	____ Other—please explain:

4. What did you do after the interaction? Check all that apply:

____ Cried	____ Ate	____ Other—please explain:
____ Pouted	____ Threw up	

5. How did you feel afterward? Check all that apply:

____ Relieved	____ Disgusted	____ Guilty
____ Victorious	____ Proud	____ Nauseated
____ Defensive	____ Embarrassed	____ Other—please explain:
____ Still angry	____ Apologetic	

6. Other memories/comments:

What We Know May Not Matter

All of us who work in libraries value knowledge, but information alone may not be useful with an angry patron. This is because people do not act on what they *know*. People act on how they *feel* about what they know. So even a library board member who knows all the policies may act angry when a staff person expects him or her to obey the rules—again the person may feel that the staff person is not showing him or her respect.

A paradox is that feelings can be altered by a change in perception which may be based on additional knowledge. So a person who is angry that someone behind her in line has stepped on her foot may calm immediately upon seeing that it is a blind person behind her. That piece of information changes her perception, which affects the anger. One medium-sized public library reported that a user became angry at staff when they told her she'd missed her scheduled computer time. It turns out that daylight savings time had started that day and she was unaware of it. Once that was explained to her, she was embarrassed, but laughed. These examples demonstrate why giving a patron a context for the situation may be helpful. They also demonstrate one way we can keep ourselves from getting angry at patrons—by seeing the situation differently (e.g., understanding that the patron is embarrassed), we avoid anger.

A Physiological Response

Extreme anger has many physiological components. Typically, anger manifests as tension in the muscles, chest, and/or head (which can cause headaches); shallow and difficult breathing; and heavy perspiration. Digestion stops, causing stomachaches. Heart rate increases, blood pressure rises, and adrenaline flows.

These physical outcomes lead many to consider frequent anger a health problem. Remember all the interest during the 1970s in Type A personalities who are prone to both outbursts of anger and to heart attacks? There is still much dispute over which is more medically dangerous: habitually *suppressing* anger (which may lead to depression) or habitually *expressing* anger (which may lead to heart attacks). The consensus seems to be that anger should be managed through appropriate communication, neither explosion nor implosion. (See more on this in Chapter 7.)

An anger management expert and clinical psychologist who writes about anger notes,

> It takes energy to be angry. . . . Too much anger can leave you utterly exhausted. . . . Research shows that as people age, they consistently report fewer episodes of anger, less intense anger, and that they got over anger more quickly. Maybe that's because the angry people die off early. Or maybe it's because those who survived have discovered one of the great lessons of life: it takes energy to preserve life. (Gentry, 2007: 342)

Perhaps the most interesting physiological response to anger from our point of view is the increased circulation of sugar-enriched blood *away* from the brain. The enhanced blood moves toward the limbs to

---

There's no need for you to be embarrassed about your past behavior when angry. A customer rage survey in 2006 found that 70 percent of consumers had experienced rage toward a customer service representative, 33 percent had yelled at a representative, 13 percent had used profanity, and 1 percent had "exacted revenge" ("For Indignation, Press 1," 2006: 26).

Men often make up in wrath what they want in reason.
—William Rounseville Alger

prepare for flight. The brain is getting less blood than usual so that it is nearly impossible for the furious person to think and act rationally—thus the expression, "I was so angry I couldn't think straight." An angry person must be calmed down before she or he is presented with rational solutions to a problem.

Anger's Siblings

It is essential to differentiate between normal anger—an emotion which can be assuaged with techniques in this book—and two of its siblings.

First, anger is *not* hostility, which is an *attitude* characterized by dislike, distrust, envy, or antagonism. Library staff usually cannot reduce hostility because it is an underlying attitude—a long-term predilection taught or reinforced by others—and not an emotional response. However, some public library neighborhood branches and small special libraries report that they have had an impact on a patron's hostility. By consistently exhibiting patience, they have taught the hostile patron to expect a positive, accepting atmosphere; the patron understands that the library is a place to relax and stay calm. Similarly, a university library reported that colleagues have had an impact on another patron. "Patience is an attitudinal factor that can be changed through the behavior and motivation of librarians. At the reference desk, we often see people with little time and patience for learning something new [including anything about technology]." How can you tell if a person is hostile rather than angry? By noting a pattern of repeated negative behavior and speech. Keeping track of patron behavior (as discussed in Chapter 8) allows staff to see the patterns which demonstrate hostility.

Second, anger is *not* aggression, which is an *action* toward another with the intention of doing injury. Aggression implies intentionally harmful behavior, which is against the law. Aggression is easier to identify than hostility because the nature of the behavior speaks for itself. Also, most people give strong signals of aggression: talking louder and faster, especially at a high pitch; being "in your face" by standing uncomfortably close to you. Usually a belligerent person tries verbal assaults and intimidation before becoming physically aggressive. Remember that you are not responsible for handling combative patrons; security staff or local police should be called in to these situations. (See more on this in Chapter 8.)

One last word on what anger is not: some physical and emotional disabilities can cause people to appear angry or difficult when in fact they are not. Here are some examples:

- A person with diabetes whose blood sugar is too high or too low may seem drunk (e.g., slurred speech).
- A person with autism may seem to be on street drugs (e.g., dilated eyes or twitchy movements).
- A person with a traumatic head injury may act aggressively or seem to be hostile (e.g., asking the same questions repeatedly due to memory loss).

> No man is angry that feels not himself hurt.
> —Francis Bacon

> Anger is never without a reason, but seldom a good one.
> —Benjamin Franklin

- A person who is a paranoid schizophrenic may be highly verbal and delusional (e.g., conversing with an imaginary companion) and make unreasonable accusations (e.g., being persecuted by the library).

- A person with mental illness who is off his or her medication schedule may seem to be on street drugs (e.g., dilated eyes or twitchy movements).

- A person with mental illness who is not medicated may seem to be on street drugs (e.g., unsteady walking or pacing back and forth).

Look at the patron's neck and wrist to see if she or he is wearing a medi-alert emblem; this can be a significant clue that illness, disability, or medication is the underlying problem. If you suspect that the patron has a disability which is causing the behavior in question, stay calm and consult with a supervisor or other staff before taking other action. (See more on this in Chapter 5.)

The dictionary is full of synonyms for anger because it comes in so many forms. The difference between frustrated and furious is really only one of degree. The angrier the person, the higher the heat in the thermometer (see Figure 1.1). The higher the heat, the more intense the conflict. The more intense, the more we tend to personalize it and escalate the situation.

> Anger blows out the lamp of the mind.
> —Robert Green Ingersoll

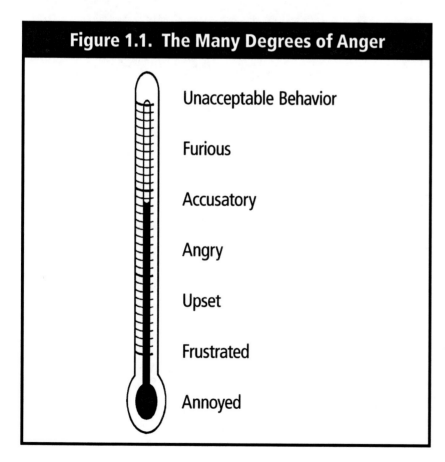

Figure 1.1. The Many Degrees of Anger

Unacceptable Behavior

Furious

Accusatory

Angry

Upset

Frustrated

Annoyed

This book discusses all of these degrees of anger and presents approaches for dealing with each of them. Anger has been likened to a raging fire, which needs oxygen to keep it burning. You can decide whether to be that second source of oxygen.

QUICK REVIEW

Understanding Anger

- Anger is a *protective mechanism* resulting from stress. To defuse anger, we need to lower the patron's stress level.
- Anger is a *secondary emotion* masking some other feeling, usually a loss of self-esteem, embarrassment, or fear. To dissipate anger we need to respond to the primary emotion.
- People do not act on what they know but on how they *feel* about what they know. So the patron's feelings are paramount in any exchange.
- Anger is bad for our health.
- Anger causes blood to flow *away* from the brain, so an angry person does not think rationally. To solve the patron's problem, we must allow time for blood to return to the brain.
- Hostility and aggression are *not* the same thing as anger and cannot be handled with the same techniques.
- Some disabilities can mimic angry behavior.

Preventive Measures

Some days it seems that many patrons are angry before they even enter the library, but that's probably inaccurate. Certainly most patrons arrive at the library in a calm and civilized manner, and if they become angry patrons it is because one or more of their expectations were not met. Other patrons do arrive at the library already frustrated; one look at their faces and you can tell that you have ready-made angry patrons. A communications expert opines that "a new attitude and a segment of American society has emerged—the *'Fed-Ups.'* In the past, the discontented constituted merely a slice of the population. Today, the Fed-Ups are nearing a majority of the population" (Luntz, 2007: 199). These people are perpetually frustrated and are on the expressway to irate. (See more on types of anger in Chapter 1.)

Whether patrons arrive at the library content or discontent, we should take action to prevent angry encounters. We can keep the first type of patrons calm, and can avoid escalating a frustrated patron into a furious one, with **good customer service skills**. The Fairfax County (VA) Public Library reports, "We have a customer service philosophy, not a problem behavior philosophy" (Waller and Bangs, 2007: 28).

If staff act positively and proactively, most patrons can be satisfied and many confrontations avoided. Users are satisfied when they feel that the quality of both the tangibles (such as materials, buildings, and programs) and the customer service are excellent. Of the two (tangibles and service), service is usually the most important to patrons. One interesting library study (Leland and Bailey, 1995) demonstrated that patrons who found the material they needed and who were treated efficiently and politely by circulation staff rated the library as satisfactory, while patrons at the same library who had the identical experience—*except* that the staff member smiled at them—rated the library as excellent.

The American Library Association's (ALA) "Guidelines for Behavioral Performance of Reference and Information Service Providers" states, "In all forms of reference services, the success of the transaction is measured not only by the information conveyed, but also by the positive or negative impact of the patron/staff interaction." The guidelines cite research which shows that positive customer service behaviors of librarians (e.g., approachability, interest, listening) strongly influence their performance (e.g., reference) and the patrons' reactions. In fact, a researcher put the behavioral guidelines to a statistical test and found that the customer service skills correlated strongly with transactions rated as highly successful by users.

The Fairfax County (VA) Public Library in its *Problem Behavior Manual* informs its employees that "All staff must accept responsibility for preventing problem behavior. . . . All employees should be alert, approachable, and proactive. . . . Greeting customers as they enter and maintaining a cheerful, helpful presence on the floor are powerful techniques for prevention, and should be part of every library's operational procedures."

Welcoming Behaviors

Many library users find the library intimidating, its classification systems confusing, and its rules difficult. Adult new readers, people who have learned English as a second language, newcomers who are not accustomed to public libraries, and people who have had unpleasant experiences in other libraries may be uncomfortable at the library. Their discomfort can manifest itself in ways that are difficult for staff. Even regular customers may arrive upset sometimes, to the consternation of staff.

Perhaps a mother, still dressed in her workday business suit, with her children in tow, stops in at the library so that one child can get a book for an unexpected homework assignment. Or a teen, anxious and clearly embarrassed, approaches the desk to ask for health information. Whatever the reason for the patron's stress, staff can escalate it or reduce it by their own behavior. When patrons feel welcome in the library—sense that they will be helped and feel invited to ask questions—they relax and are no longer candidates for angry scenes.

Try these welcoming behaviors:

- **Acknowledge people in line.** Let the patron know that you see him or her waiting. You can do this by saying, "I'll be right with you," "I'll be with you in just a minute," or "Thank you for waiting." Alternatively, you can simply smile or nod to show that you are aware of her or his presence. As the saying goes, you only have one chance to make a first impression.

- **Greet each patron** in a respectful and friendly manner. Some staff use standard greetings such as "Good morning" or "Hello." Others move right to service with "How can I help you?"

- **Use the patron's name** if you know it. There are a few caveats to this suggestion, though: Do not call a patron by name if the person is asking a confidential question or you are giving private information (e.g., overdue fines) where other patrons can hear. Avoid using a patron's name if you do not know how to pronounce it. And don't use a patron's name if staff do not wear nametags; it can seem rude or condescending for only one side of the conversation to be on a personal name basis

- **Listen carefully and give the patron your full attention.**

- **Make eye contact with the patron.** *Soft-focus eye contact* is the term for looking directly at a person without staring. You can do this by looking at the face in general—the forehead or the chin—rather than straight into the person's eyes. Although it is tempting to continue with paperwork, or to look at the computer screen, people do not feel as if they have your attention unless you look at them.

- **Maintain a polite tone of voice and display courteous body language.** (See more on this topic below.) Alter your nonverbal cues as necessary so that they are congruent with the patron's demeanor. The more similar your nonverbal communication pattern is to the other person's, the more likely she or he will consider you welcoming and nonthreatening. For example, you and the patron should be on the same physical level if at all possible (i.e., both sitting or both standing), and if the patron is smiling you should also smile.

- **Use words patrons understand and avoid library jargon.** Few people other than library staff know what *ILL* means or what an *OPAC* is.

- **Be proactive.** Ask how you can help and offer assistance beyond what is requested. A simple way to do this is to ask each patron, "Is there anything else I can help you with?" at the end of the transaction. Adopting a trick from retail businesses, some libraries now have staff members approach library patrons on the floor or in the stacks to ask, "Are you finding what you need?" or "Can I help you find anything?"

Meanwhile, there are other benefits to welcoming patrons. Anyone who comes to the library intent on mischief or illegal activity realizes that the staff has seen him or her and will observe any misbehavior. Also, staffers are noting what each patron looks like; in case of a problem, a detailed physical description may be needed.

Positive Approach and Language

Being positive means stressing what you and the library *can* do for the patron rather than what you cannot do. Speaking positively conveys the message that the library wants to satisfy the patron and that staff are there to help. Often, staff members may respond negatively to a request by saying, "We don't do that" or "I can't do that" instead of emphasizing what the library can do.

For example, a patron who asks to take a reference book out overnight may be told, "You can't check out reference books." (Note that *reference books* is an example of off-putting library jargon.) Instead, the staff person could respond with, "Let's find a copy of this book which you can take out; this copy doesn't leave the library." Another common example is the staff person who says, "That's not my job" or "I can't do that" in response to a request. Instead, the staff member might say, "Let me take you to someone who can do that for you."

One expert in communication gives this advice:

> Eliminate the word "only" with all its negative presuppositions. Don't say "I only have ten minutes," or "I can only talk for a few seconds," or "We only have half an hour." Announce that you have ten minutes as if you were delighted about it. Your voice should carry the meta-message "I've got ten whole minutes to spend with you! One-sixth of an hour! What terrific luck!" (Elgin, 2000: 45)

Another guru states, "Simply put, Americans hate hearing the word *no*. That simple, two-letter word carries more meaning than anything else in the English language. As children it was the word we dreaded most, and as ours increasingly becomes a society of perpetual adolescents, it's no surprise that, at any age, we don't take well to being told what we cannot do" (Luntz, 2007: 101).

Here are some examples of using positive versus negative language:

When You Would Say	Try This Instead
I can't...	I can...
It's not our policy...	Usually we...
You're wrong...	My understanding...
We don't...	We do...
You have to...	It would help if you...
We never...	Today...
You don't understand...	Let me clarify...
I'm not allowed to...	The best way I can help...
You can't...	You can...
I don't know...	I'll find out...
I have no idea...	I know who can help...
I have only five minutes before I leave...	Let's get started. In five minutes, a colleague will continue with you, as my shift ends then.

EXERCISE

Positive versus Negative Language

Add some examples from your library:

-
-
-
-

Nonverbal Language

Social scientists state that only 7 percent of a message is conveyed through words alone; nonverbal language accounts for the rest. Facial expressions and gestures are the types of nonverbal language we usually notice, but nonverbal communication also includes:

- Environmental cues
- Spatial cues
- Physical appearance
- Body motion
- Touch
- Posture
- Eye contact
- Paralanguage
- Behavior

Environmental cues relate to physical surroundings and their appearance. The types of furnishings and the signage, for example, speak loudly about the library. Is your library comfortable and well lit, with good signage? If so, it sends a welcoming message.

All the other types of nonverbal communication are the direct responsibility of the people involved. The cues are two way. That is, we react to the nonverbal messages sent by patrons just as they interpret staff members' nonverbal cues.

Facial expressions and gestures are widely considered universal but, in fact, they are culturally determined. For example, Americans smile at strangers as a way of showing friendliness and signaling good intentions or agreement. In most Asian countries, however, smiling at a stranger is considered rude, and a smile between patron and staff may only signal embarrassment. Another example is the "okay" sign made with the thumb and forefinger. Although this gesture is accepted in the United States, it means "money" in Japan and "zero" in France. Finger pointing is rude but common in the United States; however, it has negative connotations almost everywhere else.

The most common spatial cue is the distance people leave between themselves and others. For instance, police officers are routinely taught to be intimidating by moving in to less than a foot from a person's face; this tactic is where the expression "in your face" comes from. Standing toe to toe is always considered aggressive. The amount of space necessary for a person to feel comfortable (the so-called "comfort zone") is related to the social relationship (e.g., family members stand closer to one another than do strangers) and to the culture. The average American will stand comfortably about two and a half feet from a person she or he knows socially and less than two feet from a person known intimately. To make the other person comfortable, it's best to stand at an angle from her or him rather than straight on, eye to eye.

In Asia, most people stand farther apart from strangers; in Europe, people stand closer. Even among Americans there are pronounced differences. African-American colleagues, for example, stand closer to one another than do Caucasian coworkers. The next time you are at an international airport terminal, watch the people waiting and note how the personal

Only 7 percent of a message is conveyed in words. Body language conveys 55 percent and paralanguage the other 38 percent.

spaces they have created relate directly to their countries of origin. When you must interact with an unknown patron of a different culture, watch her or his behavior as you speak. If the person moves toward you—or backs away from you—stay where you are and wait for him or her to reply. You now know this person's preferred personal distance; you should respect and remember it.

Physical appearance includes personal grooming habits as well as clothing and hairstyles and neatness. These habits as well as body motion (e.g., swaying or foot tapping), touch, posture (e.g., leaning toward another or standing with hands on the hips), and eye contact are all personal practices. Our own habits are so ingrained that we are usually unconscious of them—but we notice and interpret or judge them in others.

By how we place or move our bodies, we—and patrons—signal how we are feeling. Most of us lean away from someone or something we dislike. When we cannot do that, we use our arms to protect ourselves or to send a message. A former FBI agent who writes about body language says that meek people pull in their arms, while strong, powerful, or indignant individuals will strike a dominant pose by spreading out their arms. Fingertips planted spread apart on a surface (e.g., the reference or circulation desk) also display confidence or dominance. Most important: if we are not trying to dominate another person, most of us unconsciously mirror her or his body language. Most people understand the message: we are comfortable with each other (Navarro, 2008).

Paralanguage refers to all the qualities of our speech: pitch, tone of voice, inflection, rate, and volume. We all know how different even a simple sentence can sound if the stress is on one word rather than another, if it's spoken quickly or slowly, in a whisper or in a shout. For example, try repeating aloud the following simple sentence, stressing the word in italics.

You can't borrow magazines.

You *can't* borrow magazines.

You can't *borrow* magazines.

You can't borrow *magazines*.

Your vocal qualities can help you with angry patrons. To calm someone who is irate, speak at a similar rate (speed) as the patron, in the lower end of your pitch scale, and watch your tone of voice. Even the most carefully chosen words can sound hostile if presented antagonistically, and imperfect wording can be okay if your delivery style is positive. Observe others when they are talking with angry people. Do they sound annoyed, impatient, or condescending? These messages are conveyed by paralanguage.

All nonverbal communication conveys attitude and is interpreted and reacted to as such. Think of the difference between being greeted by a smile from a seated person whose open hands are resting on the desk and a scowl from a standing person whose fingers are tapping the desk, or a seated person, looking at a computer screen, who mumbles "Hmm?" in your direction. Most people interpret nonverbal behavior different from their own to be hostile, so matching the patron's nonverbal cues can be helpful in defusing an angry patron.

A communications expert opines, "Likability wins in communication.... Your greatest tool is the open face. The open face means giving as much eye contact as you comfortably can. This includes raising your eyebrows very slightly. Your face controls your voice, so when you show an open face, your voice sounds friendly. Both your face and voice are welcoming. But a closed face (eyebrows down) says, 'go away.' A neutral face (flat mask) says, 'I don't care'" (Lustberg, 2002).

Staff body language that is defensive, suspicious, or judgmental can anger patrons, especially ones who are already frustrated. Crossing your arms on your chest, placing your hands on your hips, shaking your head, or wagging your forefinger are examples of such defensive or judgmental body language. Expressing frustration through body language can also upset patrons. Typical nonverbal signals of frustration are short breaths, sighing, clenched hands, or wringing your hands. Rolling your eyes shows impatience and appears condescending. Conversely, staff body language can convey positive attitudes. For example, you can signal openness by leaning forward or standing up in greeting. Supportiveness can be communicated by nodding as the patron speaks or by smiling.

EXERCISE

Nonverbal Communication

1. Stand in front of a mirror, full length if possible. Try making the open face described by Lustberg (2002).
2. Now try to add one judgmental nonverbal cue (e.g., scowling, wagging your head of finger). Can you do both things at the same time? Why or why not?
3. Return to a neutral posture and expression. Watching yourself in the mirror, try every nonverbal cue you can think of. Which one feels most natural to you? That's probably the posture and/or expression that you use most often. What does it convey?
4. If possible, repeat step 3 with a colleague and give each other feedback. Ask "Is this how I usually stand/look? What message am I sending?"

Users convey messages to us nonverbally, too. For example, when a patron is getting upset or angrier, his or her voice pitch rises and he or she gets louder or starts talking faster. Similarly, when a patron is becoming agitated—and may turn violent—she or he will start clenching hands or teeth or begin pacing back and forth while talking.

Nonverbal cues from patrons can help you anticipate their needs. For example, the patron who repeatedly checks her watch or cell phone while waiting in line is clearly concerned about time. When it is her turn for your attention, you may skip greetings and move right to giving assistance. Another example is the patron who displays his nervousness by fidgeting, rubbing his hands through his hair repeatedly, and clearing his throat often. When he reaches the desk, you may want to be especially friendly in your greeting, taking a moment to say "hello" and to smile.

A few extra words on that ubiquitous nonverbal signal—the smile—are unfortunately necessary. Some chain grocery stores which require their checkers to smile at customers have reported that some male customers misunderstand the smiles from females, misinterpreting them as invitations. Newspaper articles on the subject have made many library staff members shy about smiling at patrons. This is one area in which each staff person must make a personal judgment call. If you feel uncomfortable smiling at strangers—for whatever reason—then don't do it. A nod can be a suitable substitute, as can nonsmiling soft focus eye contact.

One more important fact about nonverbal communication from another communications expert: If there's a conflict between the content of your message and the tone of your voice, people are more likely to believe your voice. If there's a conflict between your voice and your nonverbal cues, people will likely believe the nonverbal behavior (Thompson and Jenkins, 2004).

Policies and Procedures

More often than not, the library's policies and procedures inadvertently trigger a patron's unexpected anger. Direct service staff must then calm the patron while upholding the policy. Staff from libraries all over the United States report that they have to explain conflicting, rigid, outdated, or clumsy policies to frustrated patrons.

Often these policies built up over time. Perhaps they were thoughtful and appropriate originally but have been amended numerous times as conditions and conventions change. Are the policies still relevant? Look at your library's policies and procedures and ask yourself: "Is this customer-friendly?" If the policy is protective of the library rather than proactive for the patron, is there a compelling reason? For instance, is it necessary to restrict patrons to only three books at a time? Many libraries are revisiting sacrosanct rules governing overdue fines and (lack of) eating in the library to see if they are truly essential for the library's operations. If they are not, libraries are revising them.

The library's policies should reflect the library's values, mission, and principles. If a library has a mission to serve all of the town's residents, the policy and process for obtaining a library card should not be draconian. If a library states that it values access to information, the policy and process for using interlibrary loan should make such access easy and inexpensive.

Having good policies is not sufficient. A library must also have objective standards and fair enforcement. In order to ensure that they do, the library must also have a procedure manual so that all staff members know how to uphold the policies equally and impartially. For more on policies and procedures, see Chapter 8.

EXERCISE

Philosophy versus Practice

What examples can you think of where your library's philosophy and policies are out of sync?

-

-

-

-

Signage

Some libraries, borrowing from the retail sector, are using signs to prevent certain common frustrations in patrons. For example, posting signs which:

- alert patrons to specific loan periods and any unusual lending rules, such as fee-per-use items;
- list items patrons need to speed up the lines at circulation or application (e.g., "Please have your library card out and ready" or "Please have two forms of identification such as driver's license and . . ."); and
- apologize for delays and prepare the patron for them (e.g., "Thank you for your patience. We will help you as soon as possible," or "The computer is down; all transactions are being done by hand. We are sorry for the inconvenience.").

All libraries should have patron behavior policies and library hours posted, too.

Studies show that 68 percent of people who do not return to a business or service say that the reason was rude or indifferent staff behavior rather than dissatisfaction with the product or service itself (Hartley, 1998).

Staff Attitudes

The dictionary definition of *attitude* is a state of mind, influenced by feelings, thoughts, and tendencies toward certain behavior. But *Attitude* is slightly different; when someone says, "She sure has an attitude," we know the reference is to something unpleasant. Unfortunately, library staff—and everyone else—have both kinds of attitudes and display them at work. Here are some examples:

- The reference librarian who thinks, "Kids are a pain in the neck," as a ten-year-old approaches the desk.
- The circulation assistant who thinks, "Oh, no, it's Mr. Garcia; he's always a grouch."

- The library technician who thinks, "Here comes that neurotic technophobe who can't use a computer without holding my hand."
- The page who thinks, "It's not my fault if these books are out of order since I wasn't even here yesterday."

All of the library employees in these examples demonstrate negative attitudes by labeling, avoiding responsibility, and placing blame. Labeling patrons as "difficult" makes it easier to dismiss them as beyond help rather than seeing such people as the main reason for libraries (and library staff) to exist.

Another negative attitude commonly held by library staff—but rarely discussed—is a sense of superiority. As Gentry (2007: 343) notes, "Thinking of yourself as superior to other people is an open invitation to anger. Anger tends to flow downward toward those regarded as inferior." How many times have you heard colleagues refer to certain patrons as stupid? Superiority is related to narcissism or having a grandiose opinion about yourself. Thinking that you are better or smarter than others leads to a perfect excuse to provide poor customer service: "They—the lesser people—deserve whatever they get."

Preconceived notions (prejudices) held by staff can lead them to demonstrate the very behaviors that library users commonly complain about, such as these:

- Not acknowledging people approaching the desk
- Referring them to someone else (sometimes multiple times)
- Interrupting patrons' explanation of what they need
- Making assumptions about what the patron needs
- Implying that they aren't trying hard enough and are asking for help too readily
- Sending the patron to a book or website and not following up to see if they were able to find and use it
- Trying to get the patron to accept information that's not what he or she needs
- Suggesting that the material that they are seeking is unimportant or unworthy
- Ending the transaction prematurely—before the patron has gotten all that he or she needs
- Implying that the staff person's time is more valuable than that of the patron

These judgmental positions, personal implications, and negative attitudes can create angry users or turn slightly frustrated users into irate ones. Ironically, on the other hand, upset patrons cause frustration in library staff. In a study of a university library reference staff, 70 percent of respondents said that "difficult/problem patrons" make them feel inadequate and incompetent, 70 percent said they feel frustrated, and 50 percent acknowledged they themselves felt angry and irritated by difficult/problem patrons (Osa, 2002: 260).

If you find yourself falling into habitual negative thoughts about patrons and work, try these approaches:

- Focus on now, not on past situations.
- Try goodwill.
- Use empathy; try to see from the patron's point of view.
- Focus on positive outcomes.
- Examine your prejudices toward groups of people and styles of presentation.

Negative feelings and prejudices usually show up in our language or our body language and the patron can sense it. As the saying goes, "The attitude you send out is usually the one you get back."

EXERCISE

Staff Attitudes

1. What negative attitudes do you or your coworkers bring to work?

-
-
-
-

2. What names do you call difficult patrons (under your breath or to your colleagues)?

-
-
-
-

In addition to negative preconceived notions, staff—because they are human—think first about their own situation while patrons have a different perspective. For example, faced by a patron who demands an unusual amount of time and attention, a staff member may think, "I don't have time for this. I have a report to finish before I can go home, and I don't want to work overtime today." The patron—also human—senses resistance from the librarian and thinks, "This person doesn't want to help me; I should go elsewhere." It's not a question of whose perception is more accurate or important. The patron's perception determines, in the short run, whether he or she becomes angry. In the long run, it determines whether he or she becomes a regular and satisfied library user.

Staff Training

One way to assist staff in changing and monitoring their attitudes, and to teach staff new techniques for defusing anger, is training. All staff members who interact with the public —from the janitor and the page to the substitute circulation clerk, the reference librarian, youth services librarian, and the library director—should have ongoing training.

Such staff training should be mandatory. Ironically, people who most need assistance on rethinking attitudes and on working with angry patrons are usually the least likely to voluntarily attend training. Library management should require all staff to participate in training at least once a year.

Training topics should include:

- Customer service
- Listening skills
- Library security
- Communication skills

- Telephone and online behavior
- Cross-cultural communication
- Anger management
- Emergency procedures

The American Library Association's "Guidelines for the Development of Policies and Procedures Regarding User Behavior and Library Usage" states that "training to develop empathy and understanding of the social and economic problems of some users" should also be included.

EXERCISE

Staff Training

What other areas should be covered in staff training? What else do you need to learn about or to do?

-
-
-
-

Patron Expectations

Exemplary customer service is defined as filling—or exceeding—customer expectations. So we must know what their expectations are. Libraries which focus on customer service do periodic user surveys and focus groups to ascertain their users' needs and wishes. Assuming that staff knows what patrons expect is a common and serious mistake. Patrons' typical library expectations include:

- Ease of use
- Competent staff
- Accurate information
- Availability of desired print materials
- Free Internet access
- Generous loan periods
- Access to electronic resources
- Private and confidential transactions
- Safe, quiet facilities
- Patient, courteous, and helpful staff

Depending on the library and its location and clientele, users might also expect:

- Multilingual staff
- Materials in many languages and many formats
- Unlimited loan periods for print materials
- Availability of tax and other government forms
- Sufficient computer stations with Internet access, loaded with popular software packages (such as word processing)
- Ability to print from the computer
- Sufficient power outlets for people to plug in their own laptops
- Availability of community meeting rooms
- Areas designated for quiet study and for teens
- Cutting-edge technology
- Storytime and other programs for young children
- Homework help for school-age children
- Job and career resources
- Books by mail
- 24-hour remote access to the library catalog and databases
- Convenient, free parking

Libraries of all types and sizes report that it is increasingly difficult to meet user expectations. In part, this is because of the "tyranny of the urgent," which has created an expectation of immediate services available 24 hours a day. For example, overnight mail was superseded by fax, then by e-mail, and then by instant messaging (IM) or texting for users expecting instant response. A 2009 Datamonitor survey of consumers across 17 countries found that less than half of customers are satisfied with their work–life balance, and that multiple demands on their time have contributed to the feeling of "time deprivation": "People are looking

---

EXERCISE

User Expectations

1. What are some other expectations your users have for your library?

-
-
-
-

2. How do you know that the expectations you have listed are accurate?

> When we think we are using language, language is using us.
> —Deborah Tannen

for speed and convenience and any service that allows them to feel more in control of their time." Another 2009 survey (by Beagle Research), this one of American consumers, found that more than 30 percent of people who visit a business or service expect instant attention—even if they don't have an appointment! Contrast this finding with a study of a university library's reference staff, which found that 90 percent describe "problem patrons" as those who "want an answer instantaneously and get frustrated with any delay" (Osa, 2002: 269).What they consider problem behavior is actually common American expectation.

In some communities, patrons have not only expectations but also a sense of entitlement. Feeling entitled to superior service or specific staff behaviors requires staff to feel obliged to provide it. This can translate into a very difficult situation and anger on the part of both patron and staff. For example, if an entitled patron doesn't get the attention expected, she or he will be angry. Meanwhile, the staff person is angered at the patron's expectations and attitude.

To further complicate matters, consumers do not always state, or even consciously know, how much they expect. A telling study by the Federal Aviation Agency in 1999 showed that the airlines in the United States had no fatalities at all in 1998 and fewer lost bags than in previous years, but the airlines received more complaints than ever before. If people expected only to get where they were going safely and with their luggage, they should have been pleased. But they expected more than that; they wanted complimentary delicious meals, comfortable seats, pleasant flight attendants, and on-time arrivals. In 2010, according to the FAA, airline customer complaints were at their highest even though still fewer bags were lost and flyers had been taught to lower their expectations: no free food at all, charges for checking luggage, crowded flights, and crew understaffing. What are passengers complaining about? Customer service.

Library customers feel the same way. A great irony is that people can use the library and leave satisfied even if they did not get what they wanted (e.g., a certain book). How? *If* their other expectations—especially of good customer service from friendly proactive staff—are met. This is why customer service can be seen as preventing angry customers: If none of a patron's expectations are met, she or he will be frustrated. But if the service from staff meets or exceeds expectations, the empty-handed patron may still leave the library smiling.

Patron Feedback

One realistic patron expectation is that his or her opinions will be valued. To convey the library's interest in hearing from patrons, many provide suggestion boxes in the library and/or virtual suggestion boxes on the library's webpages or blogs. It is essential that library administration respond to every rational comment in the real or virtual suggestion box. Otherwise, the library belies its intended purpose—not responding sends the message that patron opinions are not valued (or read). In many libraries, the suggestions and the library's response are posted on a public bulletin board in the actual library and/or on the website.

In addition to suggestion boxes, some service-oriented libraries use feedback cards—both in paper and electronic form—that are distributed proactively (see Figures 2.1 and 2.2). Rather than wait for feedback from patrons who are especially dissatisfied or pleased, these cards are distributed on a set schedule to every patron in the library or on the website (e.g., during one week each year). Another difference between these feedback forms and traditional complaint forms is that they encourage positive comments as well as negative ones. Also, they often ask specific questions of the patrons about their experience, rather than the open-ended questions implied by a blank card. A variation is "applause forms" which specifically elicit compliments from patrons (see Figure 2.3).

No matter how the users' suggestions, complaints, comments, and compliments are collected, they should serve as an agenda for an all-staff meeting.

Figure 2.1. Sample Complaint Form

We appreciate the opportunity to improve our services, and appreciate your taking the time to share your comment, suggestion, or criticism with us. Please complete a separate form for each comment.

Name: _____

Address: _____

_____

Phone number: Work _____   Home _____

Are you a library cardholder?   Yes _____   No _____

Do you represent yourself _____ or a group _____?

Name of the group you represent: _____

Branch, department, or individual staffer you are writing about: _____

Please state your complaint or suggestion, using the back of the page if you need more room.

When did this issue arise?   Date _____   Time _____

Are you aware of the library's policy on this issue?   Yes _____   No _____

Did you speak to the department or branch head about this issue?   Yes _____   No _____

If so, whom? _____   When? _____

What response did you receive?

Have you complained about this issue in the past?   Yes _____   No _____   When? _____

What response did you receive?

What do you want to happen as a result of submitting this form?

Signature: _____   Date: _____

For staff use only:

Staff member receiving form: _____

Date: _____

Response/resolution:

Figure 2.2. Sample Comment Form

We strive to provide excellent service and welcome comments that will help us meet your needs. Thank you for taking the time to tell us what you think about your experience here today. Please complete a separate form for each comment.

Date and time: _____

Location (i.e., branch or department): _____

Name of staffer involved: _____

Are you a library cardholder?   Yes _____ No _____

If you would like to receive a response, please provide the information below.

Name (optional): _____

Address (optional): _____

Phone number (optional): _____

COMMENT:

For staff use only:

Staff member receiving form: _____

Date: _____

Response/resolution:

Figure 2.3. Sample Applause Form

We are committed to providing excellent service to our users. Please help us recognize our best staff members. Who was especially helpful or friendly to you today?

Date and time: _____

Location (i.e., branch or department): _____

Name of staff person: _____

What happened that led you to complete this form?

Are you a library cardholder?   Yes _____ No _____

If you would like to receive a response, please provide the information below.

Name (optional): _____

Address (optional): _____

Phone number (optional): _____

QUICK REVIEW

Preventing Anger

To keep contented patrons calm and to refrain from escalating a frustrated patron into anger, try the following tips:

- Be welcoming by acknowledging people waiting, listening carefully, making soft-focus eye contact, and being proactive.
- Be positive in your approach and in your choice of wording.
- Watch your own paralanguage and that of the patron's.
- Display and distribute customer behavior policies.
- Consider whether library policies and procedures accurately reflect the library's goals and philosophy.
- Train all staff in the library's policies and procedures for handling patron misbehavior.
- Use signage to prevent common irritants.
- Watch your own negative attitudes and thought patterns.
- Be aware of body language and other nonverbal cues—both yours and those of the patrons.
- Know what your patrons' expectations are.
- Collect and discuss both positive and negative feedback from patrons.
- Practice good customer service.

How to Do It: 25 Basic Strategies for Defusing Anger

This chapter presents 25 basic approaches for coping with angry patrons. As you consider each technique, think back on the exercise you did at the end of Chapter 1 in which you recalled your own experiences responding to angry people as well as being angry yourself.

EXERCISE

Think About It

When an angry patron blows off steam, what are the ideal results? How do you want the encounter to end? Record your ideas.

The angry patron will:

-
-
-
-
-
-

I will:

-
-
-
-
-
-

The only way to get the best of an argument is to avoid it.
—Dale Carnegie

Each of the 25 strategies outlined in this chapter can be used alone. But as Ross and Dewdney (1999: 85) point out in teaching communication skills:

> Achieving a goal usually will require the use and combination of several skills. Although the process of learning a new skill requires you to focus on only one skill at a time, the effective use of new skills depends on your ability to draw on a range of skills for the purpose of achieving one goal. You may even overlap skills.

Indeed, you may find that you need to braid together a number of the basic strategies during an encounter with an upset patron. If so, as soon as you have a minute to yourself, jot down a few notes on what you did so that you can repeat it next time or share it with your colleagues.

Coping with an angry patron is not a win-lose situation; both parties should win. Both you and the patron should finish the encounter with your self-respect intact. Both should feel that you've agreed on a solution to the problem which caused the patron's anger. The patron should feel better about the library both because of the way the encounter was handled and because of the resolution. And you should feel calm and in control.

Strategy 1: Set the Tone for the Exchange

Greet the irate person in a calm, friendly voice, using the patron's name if possible. Typically, when a patron enters the library already angry, clearly frustrated, or looking for a fight, staff members hide. They leave their desks or busy themselves behind papers, hoping the patron will disappear. Actually, these nonverbal cues signal avoidance, which only makes the patron angrier.

By greeting the person in a relaxed fashion, you set the tone for the interaction. Keep in mind that the first speaker usually establishes the mood of an encounter. By acting friendly, you are providing a pleasant atmosphere, which lowers the patron's stress level as well as signaling that you expect a friendly exchange.

By giving the patron your full attention (rather than looking at the computer) and calling a person by his or her name, you are showing respect, which raises the patron's self-esteem. (For more on this, see Strategies 5 and 7.) In fact, pundits say that an individual's favorite word is his or her own name and that people interrupt their own thought processes and pay attention when they hear their own name spoken. Another advantage of calling patrons by name is that people are often embarrassed to be "misbehaving" (acting angry), so they hide behind anonymity, which is shattered by your recognition of them. In this case, the person will try to "be on best behavior" because you know her or him.

A caveat about using a patron's name is necessary. As valuable as it can be, in some instances using a name can cause you trouble. Don't use the person's name in the following situations:

- If the patron won't know how you know his or her name
- If there are issues of privacy or confidentiality
- If you don't know how to pronounce the name correctly

Believe it or not, sometimes a visibly upset patron is completely calm by the time he or she begins to speak—just by the staff person's taking the initiative and setting the tone. How does staff at your library greet patrons? A simple "Hello" or "Good morning" is sufficient, though many libraries now use greetings to announce their customer service philosophy. "Hello. How may I help you today?" or "Good morning. What can I do for you?" are common approaches. The most significant element of the greeting is not the text but the nonverbal messages, so be sure to look at the patron, smile or nod, keep your hands calmly and quietly down, and modulate your voice to be pleasant and of moderate volume and pitch.

If a patron approaches with a routine matter that you realize may be upsetting (such as paying a fine), after greeting him or her, signal that the matter is an everyday occurrence. This tells the patron that you do not consider fines to be embarrassing or a reflection of anything other than an overdue book. As the head of circulation at a suburban public library related:

> A key for us [with angry patrons is] to relay the information in a very matter-of-fact way. "You owe $4.20. Would you like to pay that now?" or "You have an outstanding balance of $19.50 we need to clear up before I can check you out today." It's critical not to have an implied judgment in your voice or in what you say.

Similarly, an academic librarian reports that it's essential to avoid a "'these-are-the-rules-whether-you-like-it-or-not' attitude or a stern voice."

Strategy 2: Breathe and Count

A typical first reaction to an angry person is shock accompanied by an intake of breath, which is held. But control your reaction and remember to breathe. Breathing regularly and deeply (from the diaphragm) relaxes your body and increases the flow of oxygen to your brain so that you can think more clearly. Try breathing in through the nose, holding the breath for a few seconds once the diaphragm is full, and then breathing out very slowly through the mouth. Shallow quick breathing (which is the opposite of this type of breathing) is hyperventilation, which causes people to get dizzy and to faint. Remember: it is essential to stay calm or you will have two stressed-out people to handle.

Count to ten. This old-fashioned advice still applies when a person begins with a barrage of words, particularly ones we don't want to hear. By holding your own response, you allow the patron to vent and calm down. You demonstrate respect. You let the person hear what she or he sounds like. Meanwhile, you have time to take a few breaths to calm

> When angry, count to ten before you speak; if very angry, a hundred.
> —Thomas Jefferson

yourself. And even more important, you don't escalate the situation by making a flip or sarcastic remark, which is like adding fuel to the fire.

You may want to think of this as the difference between reacting (from the gut) and responding (thoughtfully). During your countdown to ten, you have a moment to move away from your own emotional reaction to the anger (e.g., shock), to a rational and intelligent response.

By breathing calmly and postponing your reply, you also show that you are in control of the situation. The fact that the patron's anger has not unnerved you is a comfort to you and to the patron; the more that she or he is out of control, the more she or he wants to know that someone is in charge.

Strategy 3: Don't Take It Personally

A good mantra for dealing with anger is "Don't take it personally." The circulation supervisor at a major urban public library told me that all staff members who work with the public should have a sign posted at their stations: "It's not about me."

If you fall into the trap of interpreting a user's anger as a personal affront, you are accepting the role of victim. As a victim, you are at the mercy of the attacker, who has the power. But don't abdicate control. Your position at the library gives you—and not the patron—the authority and power to handle the situation.

On a more pragmatic note, it is extremely difficult to focus on solutions if you feel that you have been attacked. Most people in that condition are preoccupied with licking their wounds or plotting revenge. Instead, you must rally to act professionally. By taking an angry outburst personally, you double your work. Now you have two upset people to calm down!

> Respond. Don't react.

Strategy 4: Assume Good Intentions

Some public service staff have trouble thinking the best of (at least some) patrons. This may be a matter of cynicism or a negative worldview, or of listening to just one too many patrons act out. It may be a sign of burnout, signaling the need for some off-desk hours (or vacation days). Assuming good intentions is essential, if for no other reason than it will help you cope with the patron in front of you.

This isn't easy. When faced with an angry or intimidating patron, most of us immediately dislike him or her. Psychologists theorize that we get some self-righteous satisfaction in casting the angry person as a terrible human being. The catch is that if you see the patron as the devil incarnate, you will not want to provide good service. It is beneficial to assume benign—rather than evil—intent so we can help the angry patron and move on to someone else.

A former police officer who works with libraries opines that the most common danger in the library is our ego. When staff members feel assaulted, they will react in self-defense, escalating the situation. "Our ego doesn't allow for compromise and assumes the blame is on the other.... Don't show respect to be nice, but because it enhances your safety" (Thompson and Jenkins, 2004).

To show that you take for granted the patron means no harm, no matter which library rule is being broken, say something like, "I'm sure you don't know the library's policy" or "I know you didn't see the sign." This approach shows the patron that you are not assigning blame or thinking ill of him or her. Rather, in a matter-of-fact way, you are correcting misbehavior and upholding library policies. If a patron's behavior is upsetting another user or staff member, take the same approach: "I know you're not aware you're doing this, but you are making people uncomfortable by..."

If a patron claims that she or he has returned a book that your computer shows is overdue, we shouldn't act as if we don't believe him or her. Instead, say something like, "Would you please look again at home and in your car? Meanwhile, we'll double-check our shelves here."

Similarly, if the alarm goes off as a patron leaves the library, we usually jump to the conclusion that the patron has taken a library book. To show that you do not expect the person to be at fault, however, you might say, "Excuse me. We have to figure out what triggered the alarm. Could you have a book from another library or store that's set it off?"

Strategy 5: Treat the Patron with Respect

Has an upset patron ever told you, "I pay your salary"? This is a common retort, a way of demanding respect. In the hopes of influencing your behavior in their favor, patrons often use that line. I agree with a colleague who writes, "Many of us fail to realize that this [line] is a true statement. We serve our communities, which means we are not only answerable to our supervisors, but also to our patrons.... [T]hey deserve our respect and our best customer service skills" (Slavick, 2009).

We initially demonstrate respect by giving our full attention. Full attention means stopping any other tasks while having a conversation with the patron. You and your colleagues may know that you can do multiple tasks at once and that you have lots of data to enter into the computer, many telephone calls to answer, or several book reviews to read. But to patrons, continuing such tasks while they are speaking to you seems disrespectful. No matter how hard it is to break old habits, it is necessary to focus your energy on the patron and showing genuine interest in her or his situation.

Full attention also means establishing and maintaining eye contact. By looking the person in the eye, you demonstrate both that you are paying close attention and that you are not cowed by anger. Even if you are on the telephone or checking something important on the computer, look up and make eye contact with the person waiting in front of you. A note about eye contact: do not make the patron uncomfortable by staring, which is looking directly into someone's eyes for an extended period of time. Instead, try soft-focus eye contact, which means looking at the person's face—especially the area around the eyes—instead of straight into the eyes.

Another way we show respect is by demonstrating a belief that everyone has a right to his or her point of view. This is the opposite of setting up a win-lose situation, where one person will be proven right and one will be proven wrong. Most disagreements center on facts, semantics, or values. Factual differences are the easiest to deal with; semantic or value differences are more difficult to reconcile. A patron who is asked to relinquish his seat at the Internet station to someone else, for instance, may have a different definition of "fair" than you do. Rather than argue that definition to ensure that you win, keep an open mind and prove it by listening to the patron. Show that you are willing to take in this person's views and opinions for a while without making him or her feel inadequate or misunderstood.

Sometimes taking a neutral tone is the most respectful response. For example, if a patron is angry because the computer printer will not print, and a staff member sees that the patron is not pushing the correct button (the one marked "print"), the staffer may be tempted to make a snide comment or simply reach over and push the correct button. Instead, the staff person should avoid blaming the patron or being condescending. One way to neutralize the situation is to say something that removes blame, for example, "Many people have problems with this machine."

Many people summarize all of these techniques with the generalized directive to "Be polite to patrons." That's not a bad idea. Studies of citizen complaints found that 85 percent of complaints about police are about their (perceived) rudeness—and the same is true for librarians. In case you're curious, the second most common complaint about the police force involves tickets; for libraries, it is rules or procedures.

Less obvious manifestations of respect are adjusting your voice's volume, energy level, and rate of speech to match those of the patron. Matching a patron's nonverbal cues can make you seem more like the patron and therefore less threatening. And be sure to use words that the patron can understand (no jargon!).

Finally, respect implies authenticity. Simply parroting a memorized customer service phrase usually sounds phony and, therefore, lacking in respect. Throughout this book, sample scripts demonstrate certain principles and techniques. Be sure to devise your own phrasing so that you sound sincere and respectful.

Strategy 6: Listen

Listening is the most important "trick" in defusing angry people. Although this sounds obvious and easy, most of us do not really listen to a person who is upset. Maybe we're offended by the public expression of emotion and want to cut it off. Or maybe—because we've listened to so many angry patrons—we think we already know what the patron is

> "When I use a word," Humpty Dumpty said in a rather scornful tone, "it means just what I choose it to mean—neither more nor less."
>
> "The question is," said Alice, "whether you can make words mean so many different things."
>
> "The question is," said Humpty Dumpty, "which is to be the master—that's all."

going to say next. Or maybe we think we know the solution and are eager to share it. But if you are talking, you're not listening.

You must listen attentively to what the patron is saying. Then, when it's your turn to talk, you must let the speaker know that you have indeed paid attention. One way to do this is to repeat back what you have heard. This shows the patron that you both listened and understood what was said. If you did not get it right, the patron can clarify, and you can repeat back the amended statement.

Good listening is active rather than passive (hearing). It is also responsive rather than one-way. In addition, good listening requires understanding both the content and the feeling in a person's comments and responding to the emotion as well as the facts.

This kind of listening validates a person's worth—everyone wants to be listened to and understood—and therefore is especially important when you are trying to calm someone. Listening well is such an essential strategy in defusing anger that all of Chapter 4 is devoted to developing better listening skills.

Strategy 7: Acknowledge and Validate

Most of us who work in libraries are information oriented. We like to use our knowledge and offer answers. But an angry person is not capable of accepting information or moving directly to solutions. It is essential that you acknowledge the anger or frustration *first* and express sympathy before moving on.

There are a number of reasons for this:

- The angry patron is not ready for solutions if he or she does not feel heard and respected.

- Unacknowledged emotions act like static in any discussion, making it difficult to communicate. The static can block the patron's ability to listen; instead of paying attention to the staff person, the angry patron is stuck on how he or she feels.

- The patron may not want your solutions at all; he or she may just want to express his or her feelings and have them heard.

- Feelings left unacknowledged will disguise themselves as judgments or accusations and show up later as a misjudgment of the entire library or as a complaint to the administration.

By acknowledging the feeling and accepting its relevance, you are not necessarily agreeing with the substance of what's said or approving of any angry behavior. Instead, you are accepting that the emotion is there and that it can be an obstacle to solving the problem. You are indicating that you appreciate the importance of the situation to the patron and that you are working to understand it. By showing sympathy you lower the patron's stress level and reduce any embarrassment so that she or he can calm down. Then you can move on to fact giving and problem solving.

Validating Statements

Validating statements are the way we acknowledge the emotion we hear and express understanding or sympathy. Here are some examples:

- "You sound upset about that..."
- "I understand how difficult that must be..."
- "It *is* frustrating to ..."
- "I can relate to that ..."
- "I'm sure this is upsetting ..."
- "I'd be irritated too ..."
- "It *is* difficult to ..."

> We don't need to be right; no one needs to be wrong.
>
> —Otis

EXERCISE

Validating Statements

It is essential that you are comfortable with your words and don't sound like a bad actor reciting lines. Test out the formulas and then write some of your own:

-
-
-
-

Strategy 8: Focus on the Problem

When faced with an angry patron, most people initially react by focusing on themselves, their emotions, and their needs. "Why do I have to get all the problems?" or "I've got too much to do today without handling other people's emotions," or "Listening to this makes me so angry." It's necessary to nip those thoughts in the bud and pay close attention to the patron. One way to do this is to consciously direct yourself to focus on the patron and what he or she is doing and saying, rather than concentrating on your reaction.

Be sure to focus on the patron's problem or on his or her behavior, *not* on the person's appearance or personality. Despite many articles and book titles to the contrary, the patron is rarely the problem. The interchange you are having with the patron may itself be the problem. Or the patron's behavior may be the problem. Or a library's policy or procedure—to which the patron is responding—may be the problem.

If we think of the person as the issue and label him or her as a problem patron we are more likely to:

- Blame the person rather than trying to understand the situation—including the library's part in it.
- Make the patron defensive, thereby escalating the situation.
- Stop listening.
- Be indifferent to the outcome.
- Fall back onto our own personal attitudes and prejudices.

If you find yourself distracted by the patron's appearance or body language, ask yourself, "Is this central to the problem?" If you are still having difficulty focusing on the problem, you may need to ask questions, but beware of interrupting the patron too soon or too often.

One way to demonstrate that your focus is on the problem is to restate it. By restating you show that you understood the situation. Note, though, that understanding is not the same as agreeing; you can show your understanding without giving your agreement or approval. Restating also gives you the opportunity to reword, selecting your own words and eliminating any inflammatory language which has raised your hackles or may do so to the patron.

If the patron's behavior is the problem, you must focus on the behavior, state why it is inappropriate, and what the patron should do instead. For more on this, see the section on unacceptable behavior in Chapter 5.

Strategy 9: Concede a Minor Point

An angry person expects a battle. If you offer a concession—rather than a rebuttal—you appear to be flexible and conciliatory. This encourages the irate person to let down his or her guard too. For example, the patron who says "I have a bone to pick with you" expects you to say "I'm sorry, but I'm busy now" or "I've done nothing to you." By responding with "I'd be glad to talk with you," you present yourself as an ally rather than as an opponent. Similarly, the patron who complains about the lack of Christian fiction books on the shelf expects you to be either unconcerned with her criticism or defensive about the library's selection policies. If you respond with a validating statement (see Strategy 7), the patron sees you as sympathetic and on her side. For example, the patron expects you to say, "We have plenty of books; I can prove it to you if you want to see the latest fiction order" or "Very few people want that kind of book." If you say instead, "It must be frustrating to find that the books you want are checked out," the patron sees that you are not going to fight with her or demean her reading interests.

Strategy 10: Avoid Red-Flag Words

The vocabulary you use is one thing you have complete control over. And words are often the red flags which cause people to become angry.

So selecting your vocabulary carefully is a good place to start if you want to decrease the number of angry patrons you face.

Words, even common ones, have varied meanings to people because of the associations the words have. So the meaning of the word *devil* is dissimilar for people with different religious beliefs, and the word *government* evokes separate responses for people with different political leanings.

EXERCISE

Positive and Negative Words

Try this exercise with a friend or colleague if possible; comparing your answers is the most interesting part. Next to each of the words below, write down the word that is your first reaction, your free association. Then note whether your word is positive, negative, or neutral. Do not censor yourself; write down that first thought.

Television	_____	_____
Chocolate	_____	_____
Immigrant	_____	_____
Rules	_____	_____
Librarian	_____	_____

> In the middle of every difficulty lies opportunity.
>
> —Einstein

Most people say that *chocolate* is a positive word for them. But the associated words—such as *fattening, cholesterol, caffeine*—are negative. So upon hearing the word *chocolate*, some people have negative reactions. The word *immigrant* is neutral to many people, but its associations may be positive (*pilgrims*) or negative (*alien*) depending on geography and politics.

The exercise demonstrates that even ordinary, seemingly neutral words can create negative or positive reactions. We can only imagine some of the responses when library staff speak of "policies and procedures" or use library jargon. For example, you say "This book does not circulate; it's for in-library use only." The patron hears, "She won't let me take this book; she doesn't trust me with it." Similarly, you may say, "This book is two days overdue," and the patron hears, "He's calling me negligent."

Common library lingo such as *overdue fines* can make patrons see red. Sometimes referred to as the "library F word," *fine* is being replaced in many libraries by the more neutral word *charge*. For instance, "I see you have a charge of ten cents on your record," rather than "You have a fine of ten cents." If you know that your library's usual vocabulary irritates patrons, by all means change it. One caveat, though. Using euphemisms can go too far; I'm aware of one library that uses the term *extended-use fee* as a substitute for *fine*, and nobody understands the expression!

One simple word that often angers people is *why*. *Why* can sound judgmental or invasive. If at all possible, use *how* in place of *why*. For instance, instead of asking, "Why did you let your overdue fines accumulate?" you might ask, "How did these fines accumulate?" A second common word to avoid is *but*. How many times has someone told you "I'd like to help you, but..."? As soon as you hear *but*, you assume something negative will be said, and you stop listening. If possible, replace *but* with *and*. For example, instead of "I'd like to help you, but I'm on the phone," try saying, "I'd like to help you, and I'll be off the phone in one minute." Or use two sentences rather than a compound sentence: "I'd like to help you. I'll be off the phone in one minute."

Other common words to avoid are *should* and *have to*. Both sound as if you're giving orders (e.g., "You have to...") or making judgments (e.g., "You should..."). Instead make suggestions (e.g., "Will you please..."). Another red-flag word is *problem*; no matter how clearly you refer to the "problem at hand," people feel that you're insinuating that they are the problem. Try substituting "Please tell me what we can do for you" or "Please describe the situation for me" rather than "What's the *problem*?"

Any negative words can upset people, so phrase transactions positively. For example, try saying, "This is an overnight book" rather than "This book can't be kept out the usual two weeks." Another example: "Our loan period is two weeks" rather than "You'll be charged ten cents per day if you keep this book longer than two weeks." (I have heard both of these examples of negative wording in real libraries.)

Also avoid saying "I can't" because it sounds as if you are evading responsibility. Instead, use positive words and state what you can do. (See more on this in Chapter 2.)

A final category of red-flag words is the list of absolutes, such as *never* and *always*. They not only anger people, they invite an argument on the facts of whether there are any instances which belie your statement. For example, if you say, "The library never allows the public to use the staff-room phone," you are tempting the patron to mention the one time an exception was made and he or she used the staff phone. In this case, instead of saying *never*, you might say *rarely*. Substitute "This often occurs..." for "You always..." Try "Perhaps you can..." instead of "You never..."

Strategy 11: Don't Argue

Once considered impolite, public arguments are now commonplace. As Deborah Tannen says in her book *The Argument Culture*, we live "in an atmosphere of unrelenting contention—an argument culture... [which] urges us to approach the world in an adversarial frame of mind." We see this in the way our society has become increasingly litigious, with lawsuits viewed as the solution to nearly all problems. We see it, too, in the popular use of war metaphors in public discourse.

From the point of view of library service, the pervasiveness of argument makes our work harder. One of the difficulties is that when people argue, their goal is not listening, understanding, and problem solving. Instead, the only goal is winning, and some people will do or say anything to win. When a discussion becomes a conflict, facts—and selecting the best solution—become irrelevant and triumphing over the other person becomes paramount.

One way to abstain from arguing is to listen with a goal that does not put you in a win/lose position. In other words, don't allow yourself to think in terms of battle or of winning or losing. Instead, keep your focus on the goal of solving the problem, pleasing the patron, and moving on to the next customer or task.

Remember that people tend to react reflexively to the challenge. This is a result of the fight-or-flight syndrome discussed in Chapter 1. Social scientists say that 80 percent of people will fight back when they feel challenged. This is what Tannen, in *The Argument Culture*, calls "a prepatterned, unthinking use of fighting" (p. 8). But when a patron begins an argument, staff should not argue back. We want the library to have a harmonious atmosphere; we do not want the other patrons nearby to see staff arguing with people (no matter who started it), and we do not want to model that kind of behavior as acceptable in the library. So, as Dale Carnegie said, "The only way to get the best of an argument is to avoid it."

A second method to avoid arguing is to teach yourself to ignore the reflex to fight back. Remember Strategy 2: Breathe and Count. If you take a few deep breaths and count to ten before saying anything, your body will assume there is no danger and will revert to its normal condition.

Many people get sucked into arguing to gratify their own egos by proving their superior intellect or vast knowledge. Others argue as a demonstration of their power over the patron to get revenge for alleged slights or disrespect. There are two ways to avoid these pitfalls:

1. Train yourself in self-observation so you can catch yourself before you succumb.

2. Remind yourself that arguments with patrons are not personal; this is not about you, so you don't need to defend yourself, prove yourself, or exact revenge.

Perhaps the most significant problem with arguing with a patron is its implication that the issue at hand has only two sides. In fact, most library complaints or accusations have more than two sides. Our ability to see the many possibilities of any situation allows us to find mutually acceptable alternatives. In engineering, a cardinal rule is "the law of requisite variety," which refers to the necessity of flexibility in the design of machines so that the entire action of a machine is not dependent on any one part. In human terms, whoever has the most alternatives is most likely to succeed. If you and friends go out for ice cream and you will be happy with only one esoteric flavor, there are few ice cream parlors you can visit and be satisfied. If, however, you like many flavors, even the corner place with only three varieties can probably fulfill your wish. Similarly, in the library setting if staff have numerous ways to deal with, for instance, the request to borrow a noncirculating book, there is a good chance to satisfy the patron. If, on the other hand, the only answers are "Yes, you may take the book" and "No, you may not," this patron will leave unhappy. If the request to borrow a reference book is staged as an argument, the other possible solutions will never surface.

Do you have some patrons who start arguments whenever possible? Putting aside people with psychological problems or basic hostility, there are two central reasons for such behavior. First, some patrons pick fights because they enjoy the intensity, drama, and public spectacle of it. In this case, a staff member should remove the stage from her or him. By taking the patron away from the public arena and out of sight of most, if not all, of the audience (the other patrons), the staff person is taking the fun out of arguing and making it easier for the situation to be resolved calmly.

Second, some patrons argue as a way of creating and prolonging social interaction for themselves. Studies have shown that even people with language disabilities who have trouble with other types of verbal exchange will participate in arguments as a type of social event. If you feel that the patron is lonely or disengaged from others and consistently starts arguments as a way of having social contact with staff, one way to cope with the situation is to steer the patron away from a disagreement and into a conversation; for example, "We don't need to argue about this. I'd rather hear about how you liked the book." Then if the person wants to talk for too long a period of time, the staff person can use the techniques for ending any monopolization of his or her time. For instance, the staff member might give the patron a time limit by politely saying, "In five minutes I have to return to my paperwork (or whatever), Mr. Chan." Or he or she might end the interaction by saying, "I've enjoyed talking with you this morning, Mrs. Ramirez, but now I must return to my other duties."

> Dismissing the feelings that the other person is experiencing in the moment is disastrous. You may intend the message "Everything will be all right," but the message the other person is likely to hear is "I don't understand how you feel" or "You're not allowed to be upset by this."
> —Stone, Patton, and Heen

Strategy 12: Disagree Diplomatically

Angry patrons often say things that we know are factually incorrect or that we consider outrageous. The most tactful response is to say nothing at all; neither agree nor disagree and keep listening respectfully. But sometimes disagreeing is unavoidable. If you must object to something you're told by a patron, do so diplomatically.

Below are a number of techniques for disagreeing diplomatically. Whichever you use, be sure the disagreement is immediately followed by offering possible solutions to the presenting problem. Otherwise, the discussion can become a debate over your disagreements.

Fogging

One technique, called **fogging**, is to agree with any part of the argument you can, even if the part is minuscule. For example, an academic library patron says, "This library is mismanaged. Here I have to wait in this long line to get reference help from you when there are lots of library employees just sitting around elsewhere." Which part can you agree with? You might disagree diplomatically by agreeing that the line is especially long that day and ignoring the rest of the comment on staff assignments.

If you argue or disagree directly, the patron loses face and becomes angrier.

In another example, an angry public library patron feels that the library should pay her parking ticket after she parked too close to a fire hydrant because the library lot was full. After listening attentively you might say, "I agree that parking around here is terrible!" You have just established common ground, an area of agreement, and you have demonstrated your receptivity.

Agreeing in Principle

If you do not agree with anything the angry person says, agree in principle with the statement. For example, an angry patron wants the library to ban teens from borrowing DVDs because he feels that the teens are likely to damage them. You might say, "We do share a mutual concern about the care of the library's DVDs," or "Something does need to be done about the condition of the DVDs."

Scripts

Try these formulas for fogging or agreeing in principle:

- "You may be right..."
- "It's possible..."
- "You are correct in saying..."
- "It does sound like..."
- "What you say makes sense..."
- "That could be true..."
- "I can agree with you there..."
- "You have a point..."
- "That's an idea..."

EXERCISE

Diplomatic Statements

Again, you must be comfortable with the phrases you use. Create some of your own:

-
-
-
-
-

How to Do It: 25 Basic Strategies for Defusing Anger

If You Can't Agree in Principle

When you can neither fog nor agree in principle, still avoid contradicting the patron directly. Instead of dismissing the patron's statement, say, "That's a different point of view than I've heard before" or "That's one way to look at it."

It may be possible to counter the patron's comment with a personal observation of your own. For example, an angry patron wants extended evening hours and suggests closing all day on weekdays since "nobody uses the library" then. Instead of blurting out "That's not so," you might say, "That hasn't been my experience working on Wednesdays...." No one can argue with your own experience. Or just sympathize without agreeing or disagreeing: "I can see how you might feel that way...."

When You Must Disagree

When you must disagree, speak noncombatively. State your disagreement simply, following up immediately with a statement of interest in the patron's concern. For example, a patron who has had to wait in line might say, "Why do you have computers anyway? They are always down. We should just pull them out of here and go back to the old, faster ways." In this case, you could fog by saying, "Sometimes working with the computers is really aggravating," or you might say, "I disagree; usually the computers are a great advantage over the paper and pencil methods. I can see why you're frustrated by them today, though" or "I see computers differently; I appreciate the way they usually speed up our paperwork. Today has been really difficult, though."

Avoid *But*

As discussed earlier, *but* has a negative connotation. Everyone knows that "Yes, but..." really means "no." People stop listening as soon as they hear *but*. Substitute *yet*, *still*, or *and* for *but* in your reply. Or make your reply into two or more short sentences without conjunctions. For instance, instead of saying, "I'd like to help you, but I don't have the key to that room," you might say, "I'd like to help you. I don't have the key to that room. Let me ..."

Open and Closed Questions

All conversations use two styles of questions, the open-ended and the closed. Open-ended questions such as "How did that happen?" or "Please tell me more about..." encourage the person to talk and to elaborate on what he or she has already said. Closed questions, which require a simple *yes* or *no* or ask for a straightforward fact such as date or name, discourage further discussion. If you feel you must ask a question of someone during a disagreement in order to clarify the situation, be sure to use closed questions so you do not invite more altercation.

Note that direct questions (open or closed) are considered impolite in some cultures. If your patron seems offended by your question, try

> If you can keep your head when all about you are losing theirs and blaming it on you... yours is the earth and everything that's on it.
> —Rudyard Kipling

rewording it as a statement such as, "I may be able to help if you can tell me more about what you need."

EXERCISE

Disagree Diplomatically

A patron has been using the computer for a long time and many others are waiting restlessly in line. Your assignment is to uphold the posted time limit so that others can have a turn.

You must disagree diplomatically with his statements against the library, stay calm, and get him away from the computer so that others can use it. What do you say?

PATRON [*frustrated*]: I waited my turn for the machine and now I'm using it. Everyone else can wait, just as I did.

STAFF: I understand that you had to wait for your turn. But we have a policy of thirty minutes' computer time per person when others are waiting. Once the others have each had a turn, you can continue.

PATRON [*angry*]: The time limit is ridiculous. A half-hour isn't enough to get things done. I have a great deal of work to do. Since when is there a law against being a hard worker? If there are so many people waiting, it means the library doesn't have enough computers. Why don't you buy more technology instead of wasting money on best-selling trashy novels and boring puppet shows? Who's running this library anyway?

STAFF:

Strategy 13: Don't Justify or Defend

We often give explanations which are unnecessary and which appear to be offered as justification or as an excuse for the situation that has angered the patron. For example, "That printer has been giving us trouble for some time. The repair person was scheduled to come yesterday, but hasn't shown up yet." Explanations like these make us look defensive. Ask yourself: Does the patron really need to know this?

In the example given above in fogging, an academic library user commented on the apparent idleness of some library staff. It may be tempting to explain how job assignments are made in the library, but that would come across as making excuses for the supposed mismanagement. Only offer explanations if the person asks for them.

Many people want to have the last word in a disagreement, no matter what, even if that reopens the discussion and reignites the patron's anger. If you recognize this as one of your personal traits, think about how defensive and counterproductive it is. Vow to let the patron have the last word. If you can't keep that pledge, make the last word you say something neutral, like "Okay" or "Very well."

Strategy 14: Don't Use One-Upmanship

Do you ever find yourself thinking, "You think *that's* bad? You should try this side of the desk for a change"? An attitude of "I have it worse than you" is counterproductive with an angry patron. So is appealing for sympathy. Patrons don't want to hear how the computer's malfunctioning causes you difficulty. They are concerned only with how the computer's malfunctioning affects them.

When patrons have a complaint or problem, the last thing they want to hear about is someone else's trouble. For example, although telling about the library's staff shortage may be your way of explaining a service delay, to the patron it may sound like "My problem's worse than yours." (Has a friend ever said to you, "You think that's bad?! Wait until you hear what happened to me . . ."?) Similarly, comparing one patron's situation to another's can also be upsetting; for example, "All of the other students manage to get to the library when they've signed up for a reserve reading hour."

Another type of one-upmanship is assuming ignorance or stupidity on the part of a patron. "You don't understand" is a surefire way of angering a patron. "You should have known better" and "No one else has complained about this" are equally provocative, as is "Everyone *else* seems to understand that a bound periodical volume is considered a book and not a periodical. . . ."

Strategy 15: Interrupt Tactfully

If the patron appears to be able to vent forever, you may need to interrupt tactfully. Wait for the individual to take a breath—it has to happen sometime—and ask a sympathetic question that brings the conversation toward solutions. In *Verbal Judo*, George Thompson offers a specific "powerful sentence" to cut into a tirade without further angering the person:

> "Let me be sure I understood what you just said." No matter how upset, just about anyone will shut up and listen because she too wants to be sure you heard what she said. In fact, the more confident she is that you were *not* listening, the more likely she is to hear you out now, if only to prove you wrong.

Once you are talking and the patron is listening, you are in control of the conversation.

Strategy 16: Apologize

If the library has inadvertently caused the anger, apologize. Do not defend the agency or yourself, but apologize "for having caused you so much trouble" or "for the inconvenience." Don't apologize about a library rule, though, because that sounds like you don't support the policies, and you don't want to start a debate on that. No matter how tempting, never blame the situation on someone else (e.g., a coworker) or something else (e.g., the computer).

If something that *you* said or did produced the anger, apologize for it. Or, if you can't or don't want to apologize for your own behavior, apologize for the outcome instead. In other words, if what you said embarrassed the patron (who turned angry), you can apologize for having embarrassed him or her. To take another example, if your incorrect assumption about a patron's request required the patron to repeat herself, you might apologize for taking up the patron's time (to repeat the request).

As mentioned, an irate person expects you to fight back; when you make a simple apology rather than giving in to the instinct to either strike out or leave, the patron's anger may immediately deflate. The individual may be impressed that you have the self-confidence to admit that the library may have made an error. Often apologizing preemptively for something, even something minor, can steer the conversation away from the faultfinding that often develops in these situations.

Beware of turning an apology into a lengthy monologue. A good apology should simply include an acknowledgment of the fault or offense and your (or your library's) role in it, a statement of regret, an acceptance of responsibility for it (if appropriate), and a way to fix the problem and move on.

An increasing number of people feel compelled to apologize, in part because 12-step programs require it. But many people still find apologizing so difficult that the Internet is full of advice on the subject, sample apologies for any occasion, and poems, videos, lyrics, and e-cards to use. See http://www.apologypros.com for personal apologies and http://www.perfectapology.com for business and personal apologies. That site claims 80,000 customers per month. If you want to be public about your apology, http://www.imsorry.com is "an online apology community offering people the ability to apologize online, share apology stories, and send forgive me gifts and cards." A similar "open forum to post your apologies, link with Facebook, read others' apologies, and vote for your choice of Winners of the Week" is http://www.thepublicapology .com. According to *AARP Magazine* (July 2010), "overall traffic to online confession sites has increased 66% since 2007."

Deborah Tannen, the author of *The Argument Culture* and other books, notes in "Apologies Make the World Go Round" that "I'm sorry" and "I apologize" have very different meanings. She feels that "I'm sorry" suggests empathy while "I apologize" implies some acceptance of responsibility for what happened. So if the library has not contributed to the patron's frustration, it's probably best to use the "I'm sorry" formula. Remember the last time you were sick and a friend called to say "I'm so sorry you're not feeling well"? That friend was not taking the blame for your illness and was not saying that he or she caused you to be sick. Instead he or she was only expressing concern for your condition. Similarly, when you say, "I'm sorry that happened," you're really only acknowledging that the patron is upset.

In drawing a distinction between regret (focused on consequences) and remorse (focused on right versus wrong actions), PerfectApology .com raises an interesting point: "Regret is a rational, intelligent and, on occasion, emotional reaction to some unexpected, unintended . . . consequence of some event or action." People usually regret the consequences of minor mistakes or errors and apologize for them easily. But people also express regret for the consequences of events over which they have very little control or for actions that are taken for rational reasons but may produce unexpected consequences. It seems to me that a patron's anger over a library policy, for example, exemplifies that kind of situation—one for which we express regret in the name of the library.

If you find it personally difficult to give apologies, it may help to couch it "On behalf of the library, I apologize [or am sorry] that happened." For people who are allergic to saying, "I apologize" or "I'm sorry," try substituting "I wish" or "I regret." For example, "I wish the book you'd reserved had come in today" or "I regret that the book you reserved didn't come in today."

Note that *not* apologizing sends a strong message. It implies that you do not care about the patron's feelings—or about the library policy, procedure, or material that caused the problem.

Strategy 17: Use Bridge Statements

Now that the patron has calmed down, it is time to move to resolution. The way you make the transition from listening and sympathizing to solving the problem is to use a bridge statement. Here are some examples:

- "Let's see what we can do."
- "Let me help you with that right now."
- "There are a few things we can do."
- "Here's what we can do."
- "Let's try to find a solution."
- "I'm glad you brought this to my attention."

Bridge statements signal the patron that you are now going to get to the bottom of the problem and that the discussion is changing direction. Note the use of *we* in the examples listed. *We* tells that patron that you are

> If you are patient in one moment of anger, you will escape a hundred days of sorrow.
>
> —Chinese proverb

EXERCISE

Bridge Statements

Try your hand at signaling that the conversation must head in a different direction. How might you phrase a bridge statement?

-
-
-
-
-

---

both on the same side—the problem-solving side—and that you are going to work together on the problem. It also implies that the patron will be involved in selecting a solution. In the second example, the words *right now* underscore two points: that the first part of the interchange is over and that you are not going to postpone or dismiss the patron's problem.

Strategy 18: Start with Needs

It is essential to define the problem in terms of needs, not solutions. Although it is good for patrons to choose a solution so that they feel that they got what they wanted, it is important that patrons select from a list of alternatives which fit the library's policies and procedures. Often we paint ourselves into a corner by allowing patrons to specify what needs to be done rather than what they need. The first part of this strategy—offering alternative solutions—is our area of expertise and our job; the second—explaining the need—is the patron's arena. For instance, a patron approaches the desk and says, "That stupid copier in the reference room is broken again! I need you to photocopy this chapter of the book on the office copier for me." The temptation for the staff member is to discuss the availability of photocopiers and policies about the use of the office machine. But probably what the patron needs is some or all of the information on those pages. So the staff member should instead discuss ways the patron can get that information. It is very possible that using the office copier is only one of a number of alternatives available.

To continue with this example, the staff person should respond with a sympathetic statement, an apology, and a bridge statement, followed

---

EXERCISE

Define the Problem

Think of a scenario in which a patron demands a predetermined solution. How would you respond, defining the problem in terms of need?

PATRON:

LIBRARY STAFF MEMBER:

PATRON:

LIBRARY STAFF MEMBER:

PATRON:

LIBRARY STAFF MEMBER:

---

by a question aimed at discovering the patron's need. Such a response may go like this:

"How frustrating!" (*acknowledgment of patron's frustration*)

"I'm sorry the photocopier isn't working." (*apology*)

"Let's see how I can help you." (*bridge statement*)

"Would you please tell me what you needed from that book?" (*question about need*)

Strategy 19: Use the Salami Tactic

When the patron's problem is complex, try slicing it into manageable pieces. In other words, maybe a patron who has initially expressed frustration with your automated reserve system then moves on to complain about how staff are not polite enough to patrons and then to the trouble she has had getting through to the library on the phone. After listening and validating, say something like, "It sounds as if there are a number of things we need to address. Let's take them one at a time. Okay?" Then address one small part of the problem. Start with the one you feel you can solve immediately. In this case, perhaps you address the reserve issue.

Another approach is to ask the patron to prioritize the many concerns by saying "I'm sorry that you're so frustrated. What is it that bothers you most?" The risk in asking the patron to identify the priority issue is that he or she may pick one that you cannot fix or that you'd rather not deal with. However, it still allows you to work on only one problem at a time.

Sometimes you never have to address anything but the first issue. The patron may leave satisfied without making you respond to the other concerns. But sometimes you must deal with each part, one by one, before the patron is content.

> The greatest remedy for anger is delay.
> —Seneca

Strategy 20: Get a Verbal Confirmation

Once you have offered options to solve the problem—or one of numerous problems—ask the patron for a verbal confirmation. You might say, "Is this going to work for you?" This is a way to check that your solution is appropriate and reminds the user that you want her or him to be satisfied.

You also want a verbal confirmation in a situation where the options are mainly negative. For example, if you have warned an unruly patron that he or she will have to leave if he or she cannot comply with the rules, you might say, "I hope you can work with me on this" or ask "Can I get your cooperation?" This shows respect, forces the patron to acknowledge the agreement, and puts him or her in a verbal mode. If the patron cannot agree to a solution, you may mention that calling security or the police is an option. You might say, "I don't want to call the police, but I will have to if you cannot change your behavior. Do you think we can avoid calling the police?" Once again, you are asking for a verbal confirmation of what the person will do.

Strategy 21: Take Your Time

Sometimes a patron's multifaceted complaint coupled with high emotion makes it difficult to think of appropriate solutions. If you need more time, stall by asking a question. The average person can think ten times as fast as he or she can talk, so asking a question will buy you some thinking time while the patron answers.

If you need still more time, take the direct route. Say something like, "I need a minute to think about how to best help you" or even "I never thought I'd be in this situation. Give me a minute to figure this out."

Participants in workshops on defusing anger complain that "it takes too long" to interact with a patron in the ways suggested. Actually, trying to rush an interaction with an angry patron (or any patron) usually backfires and ends up taking longer. As an expert on verbal persuasion has noted:

> The most efficient way to communicate with adults who are having a verbal temper tantrum is to be still and let them exhaust themselves. Make a sound now and then to let them know you are still there.... They will not listen to you until this has taken place—meaning that anything you say to them before they've run out of steam is a waste of your valuable time and energy.... Each time you try to stop the barrage of words you will feed the speaker's anger and escalate the situation, often to such an extent that he (or she) feels obliged to start over again. (Elgin, 2000)

Also, you will need to spend even more time if the patron becomes increasingly frustrated by your seeming indifference or inability to help. And you will need to take more time, and perhaps defend yourself, if the patron makes a formal complaint to the library administration and you are called in to explain. So, take your time for both your own and the patron's sake.

Elgin (2000) explains how to use language (and body language) to control perceptions of time. "The two most important things you can do to make time spent with you seem longer... are: sit down while you're interacting with them. And avoid any movement that makes you seem to be checking on how much time has passed." If you cannot sit down, keep your body relaxed and directed toward the patron; moving your body to another orientation is a signal that you're no longer focused on him or her.

Strategy 22: Be Assertive

As discussed in Chapter 1, there are three basic styles of response to conflict: **avoidance**, **dominance**, and **problem solving**. In order to avoid conflict or to end a confrontation quickly, most people act passively (submissive) or dominantly (aggressive). Neither the submissive nor the aggressive person is willing to look (and listen) for a mutual solution and work at making it succeed. This is the arena of the problem solver who understands that the best response to conflict is to move people forward to common ground.

Passive behavior is based on the hope that the problem will go away by itself.

Aggressive behavior is aimed at getting your own way, even at someone else's expense.

The problem solver wants open, straightforward communication that will lead to a solution acceptable to both parties. She or he uses *assertive* communication to avoid confusion and demonstrate self-control.

Assertiveness is exercising the right to stand up for oneself without violating the rights of others. Assertiveness is taking responsibility for one's own actions and reactions (feelings). Assertiveness is preserving the self-respect of both parties.

When you are assertive, you stand up for yourself and demonstrate self-respect. This is especially important if you feel like a victim when patrons express anger. By being assertive you also gain the patrons' respect, and you model the behavior you would like them to use in the future.

Assertive communication is characterized by:

- The use of "I" statements rather than "you" statements
- Lack of blame or implied guilt
- Low defensiveness
- Self-respect
- Setting limits

To help you stay in assertive mode, remind yourself that you are in control of the situation. After all, you have something (a piece of information, a book, a service, a program) that the patron wants, and he or she cannot get it without complying with library rules or policies.

Let's look at more library examples. An angry public library patron demands that you allow both of his or her children (one the proper age and one not) to join the library's reading club. Although you are tempted to react and say, "Can't you read the club rules you're holding in your hand?" or "Who are you to yell at me?" you decide to be assertive. So you respond with, "I am sorry that you are inconvenienced by our club's age limits. I would like to help you, but I cannot while you are yelling at me. Shall we move over to that empty desk so we can talk calmly and quietly?"

In this example, you are requiring the patron to stop yelling. As the psychiatric social worker at the San Francisco (CA) Public Library tells staff, "Limit setting is taking the risk that you will offend the patron and that s/he will not be happy with your response. However, taking that risk is necessary... [setting limits on a patron's behavior this way is extremely effective] it helps you manage your time and it puts you in control."

Consider another example: An angry academic library patron complains about a recall notice on a book she has out. Because there are ten more days until it is due, she insists that she doesn't need to return it

> There are two times to keep your mouth shut: when you're swimming and when you're angry.
> —Anonymous

yet. After she insults your professionalism and the library's intentions, you would like to tell her to go away. Instead, you take the assertive route: "I understand your situation and think we can come up with some solutions. I will be happy to talk to you about it when you are ready."

More examples of assertive responses follow:

- "I think we should..."
- "I feel [emotion]...when...[behavior] happens."
- "I understand your situation, yet I still want..."

EXERCISE

Assertive Statements

Try creating some assertive statements of your own:

-

-

-

A few words on another assertiveness technique are necessary. Some people are taught "the broken record" technique in assertiveness training courses. This involves the calm repetition of a statement, using exactly the same words, until the angry person gives up. Unfortunately, this technique can backfire and make an upset person even angrier. The assertiveness technique offered above is closer to what's called "anger starvation." It involves letting the person vent for as long as he or she needs to without your getting defensive, recognition of the person's emotion, followed by a willingness to help and a clear criterion for obtaining that help (e.g., stop yelling). The idea is to calm down the person so that he or she can be rational in solving the problem.

Strategy 23: Don't Make Idle Promises

The angry patron assumes that you will not really care or help. All of the strategies discussed in this book are designed to convince the patron of your sincere concern and your ability to find a solution. Don't undo all of that hard work by making idle promises or giving empty reassurances, for example:

- "Don't worry about it."
- "I'll look into it."
- "I'll see what I can do."
- "This always happens."

These phrases are hollow; they offer no real promise of a solution. If the problem is such that it cannot be solved on the spot, explain to the patron what will happen next and when he or she can expect an answer.

Let's say that a patron is complaining about your library's loan period. He or she demands a longer loan over school vacation. You know that this exception can be made only by your supervisor, who has already left for the day. Rather than saying simply, "I'll see what I can do," clarify what the patron wants and then make a solid promise that you can keep. You might say, "Let me make sure I understand what you're requesting. You would like to take this book out for the three weeks between semesters? [Patron confirms.] I need to get my supervisor's approval of this. Since she has left for the day, I will ask her about it tomorrow when we open. How can I reach you to let you know what is happening? I can call you or you can stop by anytime after ten o'clock...."

Of course, there is one last step for any delayed response: you must follow through to be sure the situation is under control. In the example in the last paragraph, you might leave a note for your supervisor to see upon her arrival in the morning. Then you must follow through with her to be sure a decision is made. Finally, call the patron with the decision, as promised.

EXERCISE

Demonstrating Self-Respect

A faculty member wants a book placed on reserve, but you are unable to locate the book. Respond using calm "I" statements, avoiding blame, and demonstrating self-respect.

STAFF: I'm very sorry, but we cannot find the book. It must be lost.

PATRON [*angry*]: "I'm sorry" isn't good enough. I need that book, and I need it today. I've already told my students that the book will be available on reserve as of today. What do you mean you can't find it? It was on the shelf the last time I looked for it. Is the library in the business of misplacing books? I thought the library's job was to organize books so they're available to faculty and students. I'm doing my job, and the library needs to do its job. What if the entire faculty told the students, "I'm sorry but I can't teach today"? This is preposterous and unacceptable! Why don't you all just do your jobs?!

STAFF:

Strategy 24: Stay Safe

You must keep your safety (and that of your coworkers and users) in mind at all times just in case an angry interaction blows up into threatening— or even dangerous—behavior. Although some libraries with security officers train their staffers to call security for every dispute, more

Defusing the Angry Patron

> The more you can relieve the other person of the need to defend himself, the easier it becomes for him to take in what you are saying....
>
> —Stone, Patton, and Heen

libraries are informing customer service staff that security is part of everyone's job description. Security officers cannot be everywhere at once and cannot handle every altercation, so other staff should be trained to deal with angry patrons unless the interaction turns dangerous. See more on security staff in Chapter 8.

In our dangerous world, no one should work alone in a library building. If your library is so small or underfunded that staff must work alone, a trained volunteer should be there the entire time to act as a witness or to provide help. A coworker or supervisor in another location should check in every shift or more often as needed. If the distances are great between the library and any other library and/or the police, make an arrangement with a nearby agency or retail outlet (e.g., post office or gas station) to provide backup when necessary. Ways to contact a person there (e.g., a hotline or a walkie-talkie) must be arranged.

In a library with more staff, one person should be designated each shift as "in charge" in case of a problem. Each staff person should have a colleague nearby, both as a witness and as a person who can move in to help if necessary. You must have a way to contact your colleagues—such as with a code phrase (e.g., "Mr. Tungaraza's book has arrived") on the PA system, by pressing a panic button under the desk that connects silently to the police or a security company, or through instant messaging, which can be done surreptitiously or with the pretense of checking on something else on the computer. In addition, all staff should be on the lookout for angry patrons and should assist their coworkers when a storm is brewing. Any colleague should step in with a simple "Hello. Perhaps I can help you..."

Always pay attention to your gut instincts. Usually, your body will warn you of danger. For example, in a police study of survivors of violence, 100 percent of the people reported that they had felt the hair on the back of their necks stand up before the violence occurred.

Be sure to keep visual control of your section of the library. Often we get absorbed by the computer screen or a task on the desk in front of us and miss behaviors that should alert us to danger. Instead, train yourself to look around the area every few minutes to see if anything seems amiss. Paying attention is not just for your own safety; it also prepares you to step in to assist a colleague if you see a situation escalating.

Keep at least an arm's length away from any upset person. Be aware of physical barriers such as desks, chairs, or displays that you can step behind if a patron seems threatening. If you move a belligerent patron away from the circulation or reference desk, be sure to stay in a public area within view of others.

Be alert to the dangers of conflicts between patrons. Most libraries report that arguments over sharing computers, tables, or other resources are very common and may turn into physical fights. Do not physically intervene in such a situation; move yourself and others out of harm's way.

Never try to detain a patron who wants to leave the library. Don't block the route to an exit. Never suggest a patron go outside the building with you to resolve an issue, and never follow someone into the parking lot—not even to get a license plate number.

If you are a supervisor and need to take the patron away from a busy area, be sure to have another staff person accompany you. If possible, have the staff person who first worked with the upset patron stay with you, both to verify the patron's account of what happened and to hear what you will say.

In addition to the general rule that staff should look out for one another, it's a good idea for each staffer to have a "buddy," a colleague with whom you have made a mutual assistance compact. Remember in elementary school when each kid had an assigned buddy for emergency procedures? The idea was that the two kids would look out for each other, that in case of panic there was a chance that one out of every two would remember the emergency procedures, that there is safety in numbers. All of these precepts apply to grown-up library staff members as well.

Find a buddy on your shift. The two of you should agree to keep an eye out for each other and to be alert to difficult situations. One of your agreements is that you will step in whenever you see things heating up at your buddy's desk (and vice versa). For example, your buddy might place a phone call to you if you're "under fire," ostensibly calling you to come to another part of the library. Or your buddy might come over and stand next to you when you are handling a problem situation to offer emotional support and provide a show of strength to the patron.

However, if you and your buddy are not always in the same area, select a code word or phrase to use to alert the other. Let's say that a new area resident is angry that the library requires two forms of identification to issue a library card. If the encounter escalates and is becoming extremely belligerent, contact your buddy in a prearranged way, letting him or her know to come assist you or to call security or police on your behalf.

Besides helping you in a difficult situation, your buddy serves as a witness if things get out of control. After the fact, your buddy is someone to talk to if you've weathered a dangerous encounter. Many library workers report that having a buddy is like having insurance—you rarely need it, but feel safer that you have it.

Strategy 25: Involve Colleagues

If you feel the heat is rising and you are becoming too upset to handle the situation well, or if you think you and the patron are going in circles without a resolution, it is time to call in your buddy (refer to Strategy 24) or another colleague. Since the upset patron wants to be heard, he or she may view the involvement of another staff person as a positive step. Many staffers automatically call a supervisor in these situations, but summoning a colleague can be equally helpful. Essentially, you need someone to relieve you, and the patron needs a new, calm, polite person who may or may not be more accommodating than you are. Another advantage of calling in a coworker is the brief pause it provides, during which time the patron may settle down.

The direct and frank approach is to tell the patron, "I think you will be happier if I ask Mr. Komatsu to work with you on this" or "I feel that we are not getting anywhere. Perhaps Mr. Harmon can be more helpful. Please wait here a moment while I get him." If you are calling in a superior, tell the patron that. "I think my supervisor can solve this for you; please wait while I get Ms. Schuman."

As one veteran library director notes,

> When a person hears the same response from two different sources, he/she is more willing to accept the validity of the response. Some people do not respond to being told what to do by a female, members of certain ethnic groups or someone they perceive as not being in charge. If one is able to make that determination while working with the upset patron, make a shift to a staff member who fits the perceived "person in charge." (Turner, 1993)

Often upset patrons will ask to speak to a manager or the director because it makes them feel important to deal with the person in charge. If your manager isn't in—or prefers not to be involved—you may be able to get around such a request by saying, "If you will wait a moment, I will call Mr. Rivera." You don't need to mention Mr. Rivera's job title. If the patron insists on speaking to "the boss," who really is not available, you will have to say so but then immediately add, "I will get the person in charge."

Sometimes patrons will get upset when you call in a coworker, especially if they feel they are being passed around or that staff is avoiding the problem. So it is essential to be diplomatic in getting assistance. After you say something like, "I don't seem to be able to satisfy you; let me find someone who can help," you should bring the colleague to the patron and introduce them to each other. Then summarize the situation so the frustrated patron does not become angrier by having to repeat everything. Summarizing also gives you the opportunity to rephrase and to select the areas to emphasize. The "fresh" staff member then may be able to move directly to resolution by saying, "Let's see what I can do to clear this up." Note that the colleague or supervisor should never criticize the initial staff member to the patron but should pick up where that person left off. Sometimes patrons insist on telling their story again, from the beginning. In that case, the relief person follows the same strategies that you have tried: being sympathetic, validating the emotion, apologizing, and listening carefully, before using a bridge statement to move to resolution.

Sometimes a staff person will hesitate to call a supervisor for fear of repercussions. Keep in mind that it is the supervisor's job to help his or her employees and to step in when needed. It is best to call a supervisor or manager if you and the patron are having a serious disagreement, if you have been pulled into an argument over facts, or if the patron is accusing you of misconduct. The supervisor will then take a different tack, following guidelines for managing conflict. Usually the strategy involves asking each person to explain his or her point of view and then having each person restate the other's position to check for mutual understanding before reaching a decision on what resolution is appropriate.

> Keep cool; anger is not an argument.
> —Daniel Webster

A Basic Formula

Figure 3.1 presents a basic formula of the ten most commonly used techniques for responding to the angry patron.

Figure 3.1. A Basic Formula for Responding to the Angry Patron

Greet +

Listen +

Acknowledge +

Listen +

Apologize +

Ask Questions If Necessary +

Listen +

Bridge +

Suggest a Solution +

Get Verbal Confirmation

EXERCISE

The Basic Formula

Think of a scenario involving a common irritant in your library. Now script an interchange between an angry patron and yourself, using the formula in Figure 3.1.

PATRON:

LIBRARY STAFF MEMBER:

PATRON:

LIBRARY STAFF MEMBER:

PATRON:

LIBRARY STAFF MEMBER:

(Cont'd.)

EXERCISE (Continued)

PATRON:

LIBRARY STAFF MEMBER:

PATRON:

LIBRARY STAFF MEMBER:

PATRON:

LIBRARY STAFF MEMBER:

QUICK REVIEW

Defusing Anger

- Coping with an angry patron is not a win-lose situation.
- Set the tone for the exchange by being calm and friendly.
- Stay calm yourself by breathing deeply and counting to ten before responding.
- Don't take the person's anger personally.
- Always treat the patron with respect and assume the patron has good intentions.
- Listen, listen, listen.
- Remember that feelings crave acknowledgment.
- Validate the patron and express sympathy.
- The patron is rarely the problem; focus on the problem itself.
- If the problem is complex, divide it into manageable pieces.
- Avoid red-flag words; words can have different meanings for different people.
- Never argue with the patron.
- If you must disagree, do so diplomatically by using fogging.
- Don't justify or appeal for sympathy, and avoid one-upmanship.
- Interrupt infrequently and tactfully.
- Apologizing shows you are on the patron's side and can move the encounter from problem toward solution.
- Use a bridge statement to move to resolution.
- Define the problem in terms of need, not solution.
- Address each problem one at a time.
- Get a verbal confirmation of the solution.
- Take your time.
- Be assertive.
- Listen to your body's warnings of danger.
- Involve your buddy or a colleague if necessary.
- Both you and the patron should have your self-respect intact at the end of the exchange.

Effective Listening Skills

What Is Effective Listening?

Effective listening leads to a clear comprehension of what the other person wants to convey, both the verbal content and the emotional meaning. Such comprehension leads to a thoughtful, relevant, and effective response. Such a response leads to open communication, which then leads to a mutual understanding. With mutual understanding, two people can agree on a solution to almost any issue. From this definition of effective listening, you can see that it is a powerful tool. Unfortunately, however, most listening is anything but effective.

Social scientists estimate that we spend 45 percent of our waking hours listening to others. So we spend more time and energy on listening than on any other process except breathing. Sadly, though, the average person has only a 25 percent listening efficiency. This means the average person can recall accurately only 25 percent of a ten-minute speech after a half-hour pause.

One reason for poor listening efficiency is that our brains work much faster than we can speak. The average speaking rate is 125 words per minute, but the average language processing rate ranges from 800 to 1,250 words per minute. So our brains do other things at the same time as listening; we actually distract ourselves.

Another reason for poor efficiency is that most of us listen on automatic pilot and just *hear* others rather than truly listening to them. Hearing requires all the meaning to be taken from the speaker's words alone and doesn't allow for a full analysis on the part of the listener.

Fully listening includes three functions which will lead to a thoughtful, relevant, and effective response:

1. Attending to the speaker
2. Interpreting the words
3. Identifying the underlying emotions

To attend to a speaker is to pay full attention. To do this, you must stop all other activities and focus your brain power on the speaker, using

IN THIS CHAPTER:
✔ What Is Effective Listening?
✔ Barriers to Listening
✔ Active Listening

Hearing is what our ears do. *Listening* is what our brains do.

—Mark R. Willis

your eyes and all your senses as well as your ears. The meaning of the message is amplified beyond the words used by body language and facial expressions, so you need to observe them while listening. Sometimes, what is *not* said gives significant information, so consider that while listening. Attending fully not only helps the listener learn all the details but also conveys to the speaker that his or her message is worthy of your time and attention.

To interpret a message is to make sense of it using the cues gathered in attending as well as cues from previous experiences. Beware of letting your past experiences lead you astray—often we think we hear what we *expect* to hear rather than what was said. Other barriers to interpretation are our attitudes and assumptions, our attention span, our value judgments, the patron's nonverbal signals, and his or her choice of vocabulary. Often interpreting a message is straightforward and easy, but anyone who has ever answered a reference question knows that simple messages can be deceiving. Interpreting requires clarifying with the patron any part of the message that is unclear. For example, you might say, "I'm not sure I understand. Can you be more explicit?" or "I think you said XYZ. Is that correct?"

To identify the underlying emotion is to pay extra attention to the speaker's tone of voice and body language. Take your time and avoid jumping to conclusions. You may need to ask for clarification on the emotional element, too. For example, you might say, "You sound frustrated about this. Am I right?"

Once you understand what is said, the next step is to decide on an appropriate response. Social scientists claim that it takes the average listener 60 to 90 seconds to get to this point.

Take the Exercise: Self-Test. If you mark any of the questions with a T, be sure to read the following sections for tips on improving your listening skills.

EXERCISE

Self-Test

For each item below, mark T (true) if the description *ever* fits you or F (false) if it *never* does.

_____ 1. When I'm bored, I feign attention to the speaker. I'm surprisingly good at pretending to listen.

_____ 2. While I listen, I have ample time to determine my response.

_____ 3. I avoid listening to certain topics or ideas.

_____ 4. I know that I tune out certain types of speech, accents, or styles of delivery.

_____ 5. I concentrate on the words alone, not on the speaker.

_____ 6. I try to avoid listening to certain patrons.

_____ 7. I listen only for facts.

_____ 8. I pay less attention when a patron uses certain words or phrases that anger me.

_____ 9. I am not easily distracted because I can do more than one thing at a time.

_____10. I usually can tell what the patron will say after I've heard the first part of the message.

Barriers to Listening

As if the self-distraction of our fast-moving brains and the tendency to listen incompletely were not enough, many other barriers to good listening exist in the library. These include the distractions made by the noise and movement of other people and environmental factors such as the physical placement of the service desk and the quality of the lighting. But most obstacles are personal—ones we create ourselves.

Perhaps the most common impediment to careful listening is our belief that it is something we are naturally good at, so we don't need to pay full attention; we act as if good listening requires no effort and allow ourselves to think of other things while we listen. **Assumptions** are also widespread blocks to listening. Often we assume that we know what the other person is going to say next; we jump to conclusions based on our prior experiences. **Prejudices** and stereotyping also interfere with listening. A patron who does not speak well or has an accent, who is saying something we do not want to hear, or who doesn't look like our notion of a serious customer may not get our full attention. Our own **defensiveness** can also be a barrier; it is important to remember that library transactions are about the library and rarely are about us personally. Finally, certain words and phrases are **red flags** for us. Depending on our upbringing, political views, and personal opinions, we all have words that trigger an emotional response, which may interfere with listening.

Other common barriers are **evaluating** the speaker and telling her or him your diagnosis, as in "What you really mean is . . ." **Presenting too much information** is also a trap many library workers fall into; if you give more information than the patron can handle, he or she will be confused or you will sound defensive. **Interrupting** is another problem in that it conveys a lack of respect for the speaker.

We can eliminate these barriers by using some simple strategies:

- To keep from daydreaming or thinking about other things while listening, ask yourself silent questions or pretend that you will be required to report on what you have heard.

- To help you physically attend to the speaker, keep your body calm. For example, place your hands on the counter if you tend to fidget.

- If you tend to jump to conclusions or make assumptions, force yourself to listen to the patron's full complaint before responding.

- To avoid listening defensively, remind yourself that this is not personal.

- To refrain from breaking your concentration, eliminate all distractions under your control. For example, turn the computer screen away from your line of sight.

- If you find your attention is wandering, attend to the patron physically and your mental attention should follow. For example, engage in soft-focus eye contact with the speaker and keep your body posture erect and alert.

Thinking speed greatly exceeds talking speed. The average person thinks at a rate of 800 to 1,250 words per minute but speaks at an average of 125 words per minute. This means that we have a lot of spare brainpower to use for effective listening while engaged with an angry patron.

- To avoid tuning out someone who has a poor delivery or who has an accent, concentrate on the content of the message rather than the style.

- To abstain from reacting instinctively to red-flag words, translate the trigger word in your mind. For example, if the word *immigrant* starts you thinking about relatives who are immigrants (a positive train of thought) or if it reminds you of recent policies adopted by your state legislature with which you disagree (a negative train of thought), substitute a word that is neutral to you, such as *newcomer*.

- So that you don't put your words or feelings into the speaker's mouth, try to use sentences that begin with "I" rather than "you." (See more on this in Chapter 3 in the section on being assertive.)

- To keep information giving to a minimum, ask yourself, "Does the patron really need to know this?"

- If you find yourself interrupting, immediately apologize and allow the person to finish.

Active Listening

People always need to feel listened to. In Chapter 1, we discussed the importance of showing respect for the patron as a way to decrease his or her stress. Active listening, developed by Carl Rogers and popularized by Thomas Gordon, is the primary method of demonstrating respect for the patron.

Active listening—also called empathic listening—is active rather than passive, responsive rather than one way, and sympathetic rather than judgmental.

Active listening requires careful attention to both **content** and **feeling**. If a patron, sounding harried and looking frustrated, reports that the microfiche reader doesn't work again today, a staff person who is a good listener will respond to both the emotion (frustration) and the message (broken machine). For example, the staff person may say, "It's so frustrating when that machine is on the blink," before moving to a solution.

Active listening implies that listening and understanding—not responding—are the goals of the listener. That seems obvious, doesn't it? But most people use part of their brainpower to figure out a response, and many people interrupt to use that response as soon as possible. In active listening, understanding the patron and confirming that you have understood are the main goals.

The basic technique of active listening is **reflection**. Reflection statements allow you to check your understanding of what the other person has said. They also allow the speaker a chance to hear back his or her own statements and then to refine or alter them.

By reflecting a person's statements, you also demonstrate that you have listened carefully. This is a validating experience for the speaker—

everyone loves being listened to. In fact, the speaker will feel better listened to if your response is a reflection of what he or she said, rather than a solution or interpretation. In an active listening situation, solutions and interpretations should only be offered *after* you have reflected the content and the feeling of the speaker.

At the beginning of an exchange, just listen. Indicate that you are paying attention by saying "Oh" or "Really?" or by nodding. It used to be standard advice to recommend injecting a minimal encourager, such as "Mm-hm." But Deborah Tannen, an expert in communication across genders and author of *The Argument Culture*, reports, "Men and women interpret listening signals (e.g. 'uhuh,' 'mmm,' 'yeah') differently. To a woman 'yeah yeah' means 'I am listening.' To a man it means 'I agree.' If it turns out that the woman does not agree, the man may conclude that the woman is being insincere." So, to be careful, it's best to avoid "Uh-huh" and "Yeah" and to use short comments such as "Oh," "Really," and "Go on."

Next, pause and consider what you have heard before responding. Do not judge, argue, or defend. If you need more information, ask a question using reflection. You can do that by turning one of the speaker's statements into a question. For example, if a patron says, "I've been to many libraries looking for this article," you might ask, "You say you've been to many libraries looking for this article?" After the speaker is finished, reflect back what you have heard. (See the next section for more on how to do this.)

One caveat: Active listening encourages the speaker to continue, to talk more, and to explain himself or herself more fully. So if you do not want to generate further dialogue, stop using reflecting statements and move on to solutions. For example, if the patron has broken a library rule (e.g., disturbing others), you do not want to elicit discussion on the matter. Instead, you want the patron to stop the negative behavior. If the patron has been long-windedly venting his or her frustration with the library's policy on renewals, you do not want the individual to talk more on the topic. Instead, you want to suggest solutions.

> If you are talking, you are not listening.

Reflection

In *On Becoming a Person*, Rogers specified four levels of reflection:

1. Repeating word for word, changing only "I" to "you"
2. Repeating only part of what was said, using the speaker's words
3. Summarizing in your own words what you've heard
4. Summarizing content and expressing the feeling you've heard

The first type of response is *not* recommended for use with an angry patron, as it may seem snide to repeat the complaint exactly. The other three types are all acceptable, but the last one is by far the most powerful. Restating the content and reflecting the feeling demonstrate respect by showing that you understand the words of the message and that you accept the emotion that is present. Note that this does not mean that you necessarily agree with the content or condone the feeling, but that you "got" them both.

If you focus only on the possible solutions and ignore the person's feelings, you may intensify the anger and the emotions it covers, such as embarrassment. A person who shows her or his anger wants to be heard and wants you to acknowledge that you have heard. (See more on this in Chapter 1.)

Here are some formulas for reflection of both content and feeling. Try these out to see if they're comfortable for you.

- "It really is [feeling] when [content]."
- "It looks like you [feeling/verb] because [content]."
- "I can appreciate that you [feeling/verb] since [content]."
- "I see that [content] has caused you to [feeling]."

A word of caution here: Avoid saying, "I know what you are feeling" or "I understand what you are feeling," as an angry person probably will question you: "How do *you* know what *I* am feeling?" "I understand" can send the message "I've heard quite enough," or it can sound patronizing. If, indeed, you have been through a similar situation and feel like sharing that to prove your personal expertise, then you can say, "I know what you are feeling because I've been in the same spot." No matter what wording you use, it is essential that you sound sincere; otherwise, you will only make the patron angrier.

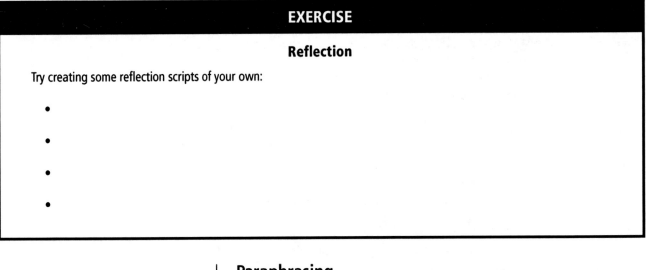

EXERCISE

Reflection

Try creating some reflection scripts of your own:

-
-
-
-

Paraphrasing

A type of reflection is paraphrasing in which you reword what the speaker said, summarizing what you think he or she meant in your own words. As Thompson (and Jenkins, 2004) explains,

> To paraphrase is to put another person's meaning into your words and deliver it back to him. . . . [Y]ou can cast what you think lies behind his aggressive words (his real point) in your own words (which will be calmer because you're not the emotionally charged

We spend 70 to 80 percent of our waking hours in some sort of communication.

one here. . . . Suddenly you have not his words with his meaning or your words with your meaning, but your words with his meaning. . . .

Sample scripts follow:

- "I get the feeling . . ."
- "So you think . . ."
- "As you see it . . ."
- "If I understand you . . ."

EXERCISE

Paraphrasing

Try creating some paraphrasing scripts of your own:

-
-
-
-

EXERCISE

Responding

A patron who has brought her preschool child to the library for story hour wants to stay with him. Although you tell her the children-only rule for children's programs, she insists on staying with her son. You politely restate the policy. She responds, "I can't believe what I'm hearing! I always stay with my son during programs. The recreation department always allows it at their programs. He's far too young to stay alone! And story hour isn't crowded today; there's enough room for me."

How do you respond? Remember to listen actively, validate her concerns, and use reflection statements or paraphrasing. Your goal is to make the patron know that you are really listening and empathizing and that you understand what she means. This may take two or three back-and-forth exchanges in which she talks and you listen. Once she realizes that you *are* listening, she will calm down. Only then can you move on to explore possible solutions.

LIBRARY STAFF PERSON:

ANGRY PATRON:

LIBRARY STAFF PERSON:

ANGRY PATRON:

LIBRARY STAFF PERSON:

QUICK REVIEW

Listening Effectively

- Effective listening → comprehension → thoughtful and relevant response → mutual understanding → solution.
- Though we spend nearly half our waking hours listening to others, few of us do so at more than 25 percent efficiency.
- Our brains work far faster than anyone speaks.
- Fully listening includes attending, interpreting, and identifying the underlying emotion.
- Assumptions and prejudices are common barriers to good listening.
- Other barriers include red-flag words, evaluating the speaker, and interrupting.
- Active listening implies that listening and understanding—not responding—are the goals of the listener.
- A basic technique of active listening is reflection.
- The most powerful type of reflection summarizes content and expresses the feeling you've heard.
- Paraphrasing is a type of reflection that allows you to summarize what you have heard in your own words.

Beyond the Basics: Difficult Situations

IN THIS CHAPTER:

✔ Complaints

✔ Accusations

✔ Unacceptable Behavior

✔ Mentally Ill Patrons or Patrons under the Influence of Drugs or Alcohol

✔ Telephone and Virtual Encounters

Complaints

Do you feel grateful when listening to a patron's complaint? According to customer service gurus, you should be. Since only 4 percent of unhappy customers ever complain, we should be thankful that they alert us to issues that probably upset many other people too. Customer service texts contend, "Every complaint is an opportunity," but that should be reworded in the plural because two opportunities are involved. The first is a chance for problem solving that may improve our service for everyone. The second is the occasion to satisfy the patron in front of us, who will judge the library not on the initial incident which caused the distress but on how the complaint was handled.

The deputy director of a public library in a medium-sized college town told me, "I always thank the person for taking the time to come and speak to me with a complaint (even if I disagree with the complaint itself). Underlying this is the thought that even for the most unstable among our complainers, there is a seed of care and concern that may have instigated the urge to communicate."

The most common complaints in public libraries are about the computer stations, especially about the waiting lists to use them and the time limits on them. Runners-up for first place are complaints about library requirements (e.g., proof of address to get a library card), library policies (e.g., no renewal if someone else has reserved that book), and library procedures (e.g., claimed return items). Angry interactions between patrons, often over use of a table, computer station, or other equipment, are also commonplace.

Disagreements between users of different age groups often lead to complaints. For example, many older adults speak loudly to each other (and to staff) due to hearing impairments. They feel disrespected if they are asked to "tone it down." Meanwhile, older adults often complain about teens, especially in libraries near junior high and high schools. Typically, some older adults have traditional expectations of the library, including separate quiet reading and research areas. The teens that come directly to the library after school, however, can be energetic and noisy. Usually, the difference in library styles doesn't become a problem if the library has enough space to allow a quiet area away from the teen area. Even then, though, there can be problems in the computer area as many older users want to search the library catalog and the Internet alone and in silence, while the teens prefer to work in groups of two or more.

The basic strategies outlined in Chapter 3 all apply to complaints. It is essential to listen carefully, sympathize with the patron's concern, and apologize for the situation. You may have to repeat this cycle—the patron may have more to say, in which case you will have to listen and validate again.

At this point, the patron should be somewhat calmed down and able to rationally discuss solutions to the problem. So you:

- **Ask questions** if necessary to fully understand the situation. Closed questions (ones that require short answers such as "yes" or "no") are probably best. (See more on closed questions in Chapter 3.)

- **Restate the problem** the patron is complaining about to show that you understand it.

- **Offer the patrons options**, if at all possible.

- **Let the patron select the solution most agreeable to him or her.** Of course, since you are presenting the options from which the patron will choose, you ensure that only options acceptable to the library are discussed. You also retain control of the situation by presenting feasible alternatives.

- **Explain what will happen next.** If the problem is not something you can fix on the spot, tell the patron what you plan to do. If anyone else will be involved, tell the patron who that is. Write down the agreed-upon solution so that you don't forget—and the patron sees that you mean it and plan to follow through. Be sure not to promise a solution you cannot deliver.

- **Ask for a verbal confirmation** that the patron finds the solution acceptable and understands what will happen and when.

- **Follow up.** If you have promised to call back, do so. If you have promised that a supervisor will call, double-check that your supervisor has done so. If you promise to mail, fax, or e-mail something to a patron, call him or her to be sure it was received. Following up on a pledge demonstrates the library's concern with patron satisfaction.

- **Call in a colleague or your supervisor**, if the patron asks to speak to a manager or if you feel that another staff person may be able to do a better job with this patron.

Sample Scenario

A patron comes to the circulation desk to retrieve a book she has reserved online at home. The staff member checks and finds that the book is not in.

> Every discontent customer tells an average of 11 others, each of whom tells 5 more. This means that 76 people are hearing negative stories about the library every time we hear one complaint.

PATRON: I don't understand. I received a postcard [telephone call, e-mail message] that the book I reserved is in. I had to leave work early to get here before you close. And now you say the book isn't in. I took personal leave time for nothing!

STAFF: I'm sorry—that must be so frustrating! May I see your library card so I can check on what happened?

PATRON [*handing over card*]: Here.

STAFF [*checking computer screen*]: I see what happened. The book went to XYZ branch, which is the default branch if no branch is specified. Should I have them send it over here? It will take about two days.

PATRON: Yes, I don't want to have to go to XYZ!

STAFF: There are a couple of things we can do to save you another unnecessary trip. I can give you a telephone number to call to check on the book before you come. Or, if you prefer, I can call you when I know that it has arrived.

PATRON: I'm pretty hard to reach. Why don't you give me a number to call—but not one that gets me the electronic system that keeps you pressing numbers all day!

STAFF [*handing her a slip of paper*]: Here's a number that will get you directly to this desk. Anyone who answers will be able to help you.

PATRON: Thanks. But why did the book go to XYZ anyway?

Figure 5.1. A Formula for Handling Complaints

Greet +

Listen +

Acknowledge +

Listen +

Apologize +

Bridge +

Restate Problem +

Offer Options +

Explain What's Next +

Get Verbal Confirmation +

Follow Up

STAFF: Did you reserve this yourself online?

PATRON: Yes.

STAFF: After you fill in all the blanks, the screen asks you to select a branch to receive the book. Many people don't notice that and don't select a branch. If no branch is specified, the book goes to XYZ.

PATRON: Oh. Well, thanks.

EXERCISE

Handling Complaints

Try scripting out a scenario from your library:

PATRON:

STAFF:

PATRON:

STAFF:

PATRON:

STAFF:

PATRON:

STAFF:

PATRON:

STAFF:

PATRON:

STAFF:

Accusations

It is extremely difficult to remember and use the basic strategies (or any strategies at all!) when faced with an accusation. No matter what the exact charges are or whether the angry patron accuses you personally, a colleague, or your library as a whole, it is difficult to stay calm and sympathetic.

Boxers say that the secret to success in boxing is to focus on the other person at all times, even when—confronted with injury—the instinct is to think about self-protection. That advice also applies to coping with an angry accuser.

Here are some guidelines for responding to accusations:

- Concentrate on the patron and what his or her **need** is. This may require **translating the comment into a request for service**. Example: A patron says, "This library never has the books I need. Who does the book ordering around here—some kind of simpleton?" Ask yourself, "What would that comment be if he or she were calm?" Then respond to your translation. In this case, respond only to the patron's need for materials. "I'm sorry you haven't found what you need. What books are you looking for? Perhaps I can help you."

- Do **not** get pulled into a discussion of the accusation itself, and **do not rationalize** or defend. In the previous example, avoid the temptation to discuss how book selection is done or the credentials of the librarian who does it.

- **Do not respond reflexively.** A typical reflexive response is to repeat the negative buzzword or accusatory label and to defend yourself and your colleagues. In the previous example, refrain from saying, "Simpleton? I'm not a simpleton!" If you fall into that trap, the other library users have now heard the word *simpleton* attached to you three times instead of once.

- Don't think aloud. Instead, **pause to consider your best response.** If necessary, tell the patron, "I need a minute to think about this" or "Wow! I never thought I'd hear anything like that. Let me think for a minute."

- **Do not answer an accusation with a question**; this invites more accusations. In the previous example, responding with "Who are you calling a simpleton?" invites "Any of you library workers who orders the books around here must need a brain transplant!"

- **Don't answer any rhetorical questions.** Treat them as statements that require no response.

- **Apologize easily.** You can always apologize for "the inconvenience" if you don't feel you want to apologize for the named situation (in this example, the library's selection policies). (See Chapter 3 for more on apologies.)

> When we blame someone, we are offering them the role of "the accused," so they do what accused people do: they defend themselves any way they can.
>
> —Stone, Patton, and Heen

- **Be positive** and speak from pride. In the accusation above, you might say "Our library is proud of its collection. Among other things, we take suggestions from the public. Would you like to recommend a book for purchase?"

- **Be assertive** and use "I" statements. It is often tempting to use "You" statements, such as "You should be ashamed of yourself!" or "How dare you talk to me that way!" Avoid this reaction. Instead, speak from your point of view. For example, "I never thought I'd hear a comment like that about our library. I am proud of all our library does for the community." (For more on assertiveness, see Chapter 3.)

- Often complainers enjoy the attention they're getting—from you and from other patrons. If you sense that this is the case, **remove the accuser's soapbox**. Ask him or her to come with you to a quieter location. Moving the patron often has the added side benefit of allowing him or her time to cool down. If you do not have the physical space to move far, or if you do not have enough staff to cover the desk if you leave, you can still try to remove the spotlight by speaking more softly or turning in such a way that the accuser turns too and is not as visible.

- Depending on whether offensive language is used, how directly personal the accusations are, and whether you feel physically threatened, **accusations may fall into the category of verbal abuse**, which is unacceptable behavior according to most libraries' rules of behavior and/or local ordinances or state law. See more on this in the next section of this chapter.

Sample Scenario

An enraged patron is speaking heatedly and loudly to a staff member because a book is not on the shelf, though the computer record says it is there.

> Feelings are very good at disguising themselves as emotions we are better able to handle.... [F]eelings transform themselves into judgments, accusations, and attributions.
>
> —Stone, Patton, and Heen

Figure 5.2. A Formula for Handling Accusations

Pause +

Translate into a Request for Service +

Apologize +

Speak Positively and Assertively +

Bridge +

Offer Service

PATRON: I just waited in line for twenty minutes, but I see lots of staff just sitting around over there. Do they hire only lazy people here, or do they train you to be lazy after you're hired?

STAFF: I'm sorry you had to wait in line so long. How can I help you?

PATRON: It would help if more staff were working!

STAFF: We are all doing our best on a very busy day. Can I help you now?

EXERCISE

Accusations

Try scripting out a scenario from your library:

PATRON:

STAFF:

PATRON:

STAFF:

PATRON:

STAFF:

PATRON:

STAFF:

PATRON:

STAFF:

PATRON:

STAFF:

Unacceptable Behavior

A fine line exists between garden variety angry encounters and unacceptable confrontations. Unfortunately, users who are angry often do step over the line into unacceptable behavior. A 2007 study in Britain found that 25 percent of computer users have physically attacked their computer in anger at some time.

The Fairfax County (VA) Public Library defines behavior that is over the line as "behavior that requires an immediate response because it threatens the rights or safety of customers or staff." Their *Problem Behavior Manual* continues,

> Customers, unfortunately, have a right to be rude, angry, or careless. We want this definition to help staff step back in any given situation and ask, "What is really going on here? Does this pose a threat?" Certainly, defining such behavior can be a challenge. For example, while people have a right to be rude or angry, they cannot be abusive. They might call library policies stupid or ask to speak to a supervisor, but if they suddenly say "You're a lying cow and you'll be sorry," they've stepped over a line.

As long as the upset patron displays anger only through language (verbal and body language) without any threat (as in the previous example), library staff usually can follow the basic strategies in Chapter 3. If, however, the irate patron's *behavior* is unacceptable, guidelines for staff response are different. Note that in some places (e.g., California), a person who "maliciously and willfully disturbs another person by loud and unreasonable noise" or who "uses offensive words in a public place which are inherently likely to provoke an immediate and violent reaction" is actually committing a state penal code violation. In those instances, language and behavior are one and the same. Cities and counties differ on the use of this law in a library situation.

For example, you would follow basic strategies with a patron who is angered by the rules for your summer reading program and *talks* to you about his perception that the policy for awarding prizes is unfair. But if that patron yells or throws down his books, you must deal with his unacceptable *behavior*.

In most libraries, "disrupting the everyday operations of the library" is the catchall phrase that defines unacceptable behavior. In some states, such as California, "intentional interference with lawful business" is actually a penal code violation. If the unacceptable behavior interferes with others' use of the library or threatens anyone's safety, security staff or police should be called. Check with your supervisor about your library's policies and procedures regarding this kind of situation.

Two other notes on responding to unacceptable behavior: First, do *not* use active listening in this situation. The primary goal here is to change or stop the behavior, not to help the patron feel better. Second, be aware of the strength of the words you use. For example, "You must..." is a much more controlling statement than "I need you to..." or "I would like you to..." And both of the latter are stronger than "Would you please...?"

Use the following steps in a confrontation *that you feel you can handle*:

- **Make a good-faith statement.** Similar to a validation, such a statement lets the patron know that you still have control of yourself and will give her or him the benefit of the doubt. For example, say, "I can understand that you..." or "This is especially frustrating. Isn't it?" After this is done, *immediately* move to the next step.

- **Label the problem behavior.** For example, "Shouting at me..." Be sure to disapprove of the *behavior* only, not the person or the emotion. If the behavior is not allowed by library policy (e.g., throwing materials), point that out. Then *immediately* move on to the next step.

- **State how the behavior affects your ability to provide service.** For example: "[This behavior] upsets me so that I cannot think clearly." Phrase your response so that it is clear that your reaction is counterproductive for the patron. Angry people do not care if they are causing you pain—they may even tell you directly, "I don't care about your stupid headache!" But angry people *are* concerned about getting what *they* want. So in this example you might say, "Shouting at me makes it difficult for me to help you."

- **Do *not* allow time for patron response** or discussion between the good-faith statement, the labeling of behavior, and the statement of your response. The patron has a chance to answer only after you've used the whole formula.

- **You may have to repeat the three-part formula.** Give the patron this second chance.

- **Suggest a method for dealing with the anger.** Try saying, "Why don't we move away from the circulation desk and discuss this quietly over here?" or "I think it's best if someone else speaks with you now." If necessary, say, "I will help you when you can speak to me without shouting."

- **Work toward a solution to the problem** by focusing on the patron's need in the context of the library's rules. Stress the positive; for example, "Let me show you an area where you can smoke," rather than "You are not allowed to smoke here."

- **If necessary, repeat the rule in question**—without being defensive or apologetic.

- **Be assertive.** Use direct "I" statements that are clear, concrete, and consistent. (For more on assertiveness, see Chapter 3.)

- If these methods are not effective in stopping the problem behavior, **give the patron one last option**: Discontinue the behavior or leave the library. If the person leaves, do not follow him or her out of the library for any reason.

- If you feel at risk (e.g., the hair on the back of your neck stands up), **move to an area with a physical barrier between you and the patron** (e.g., a desk or counter) and where there are other coworkers. Be sure to stay in a visible public area; do not move to an enclosed area as the patron may follow you.

- **If necessary, call security or the police**. It is wise to prearrange a code phrase with your coworkers so that they know when you want the police to be called. For example, you may say to a colleague, "Please get Mr. Berman; he will know what to do." In this example, your colleagues know that "Mr. Berman" is your internal code for "Call the police." (Staying safe is discussed in more detail in Chapter 3.)

- If the patron understands that you are calling security or the police and starts to leave the library, let him or her go. **Do not try to keep the patron from leaving**.

Sample Scenario

A visibly angry patron approaches the reference desk and throws down a reference book.

PATRON [*screaming*]: *Every time* I come to this library something's screwed up!

STAFF: I'm sorry you feel that way. Let's see if...

PATRON [*screaming, interrupting staff person*]: Sorry, schmorry! What about my report?

STAFF: I'd like to help you. Yelling makes it hard for me to find solutions. If you can calmly tell me more about this, I can try to help.

Figure 5.3. A Formula for Handling Unacceptable Behavior

Make Good-Faith Statement +

Label Problem Behavior +

State Your Response to It +

Suggest Solution +

Repeat Rule +

Repeat Solution +

Get Verbal Confirmation +

Call Security or Police

PATRON [*screaming*]: Something's *always* broken around here. Today it's the photocopy machine, and I have to copy this to do my report!

STAFF: As I said, I really want to help, but yelling makes it impossible. Please lower your voice so we can discuss this.

PATRON [*quieter*]: Can you really do something? I have to have this information right away!

STAFF: I have a few ideas. One possibility. . .

EXERCISE

Unacceptable Behavior

Try scripting a scenario from your library:

PATRON:

STAFF:

PATRON:

STAFF:

PATRON:

STAFF:

PATRON:

STAFF:

PATRON:

STAFF:

PATRON:

STAFF:

Mentally Ill Patrons or Patrons under the Influence of Drugs or Alcohol

Many library staffers bemoan the number of mentally ill people who visit the library and assume that many of the incidents of public anger involve those people with mental illness. A recent study on this topic (Torrey, Esposito, and Geller, 2009: 49), however, found that less than 10 percent of mentally ill people—almost all of whom are untreated for their psychiatric disorders—cause problems in community facilities such as parks, transit stations, and libraries. "The great majority of people with serious psychiatric disorders use public libraries appropriately without causing problems."

If you suspect a patron is mentally ill or is under the influence of drugs or alcohol, be wary. Such patrons may exhibit sudden and extreme mood changes. Clues that a person may be under the influence include slurred speech, pacing back and forth, unsteady walking, irrational speech, and dilated pupils. Another indicator of alcohol abuse is being able to smell alcohol on the patron's breath. (See more on this in the Anger's Siblings section of Chapter 1.) Take a look at the patron's jewelry: People who have recently been released from the hospital often wear medical alert identification bracelets or necklaces.

If patrons display behaviors typical of substance abuse or mental illness but do not seem ill and are not bothering anyone, there is no need to approach them. But if their behaviors are disturbing other patrons, or if they appear to be sick, you must talk to them. If possible, bring a coworker with you. Ask "Are you okay?" or "Do you need medical assistance?" Call for an ambulance if a patron needs help. If the person does not want medical assistance or does not seem ill, focus on the disruptive behavior as you would with any other patron. Follow the steps given for unacceptable behavior earlier in this chapter and the tips that are provided later in this chapter.

Library staffers frequently report feeling overwhelmed when dealing with a patron who is mentally ill or under the influence of drugs or alcohol. Sometimes they are frightened by people who seem so different from them. On the other hand, sometimes they are frightened by how similar mentally ill or addicted people are to their relatives or themselves. Sometimes they feel guilty because they do not like being with people who are mentally ill or under the influence. Leah Esguerra, MFT, a psychiatric social worker at the San Francisco (CA) Public Library, reminds staff that "it is okay to not like some of the patrons."

Often a patron who seems mentally ill or under the influence will try to monopolize the time and attention of another library user or a staff member. As an experienced public library branch manager suggests, you should disengage from the patron and redirect him or her to something else. In other words, do not get pulled into a discussion of anything but a rational library-related need. Here are a few tips:

- **Project a sense of calm**—even if you do not feel it—to show that you are in control of the situation. The more the person feels out of control, the more important it is to him or her that someone is in charge. That someone is you.

- **Do not corner or touch** the patron. Often physical attacks stem from an attempt to protect personal space rather than to injure others.

- **Do not go alone** with the patron to a remote area of the library (e.g., stacks).

- **Do not treat the person condescendingly**; being mentally ill or under the influence does not mean the person is stupid.

- **Do not argue** with outrageous statements, delusions, or hallucinations.

- **Redirect the patron** toward something library related and rational whenever possible.

- **Be assertive and firm**—not apologetic or defensive—about issuing warnings on unacceptable behavior.

- **Be direct and concise** in any requests or instructions. Repeat them if necessary.

- **Most patrons are not dangerous.** But if you feel uncomfortable or know that the patron has unpredictable extreme mood changes, do not handle the situation alone; involve a coworker. Be wary of appearing confrontational, though, with what might appear to be a show of force.

- **Walk away if you feel at risk.** Listen to your instincts on this one and do not put yourself in any danger. Walk away slowly and calmly, as running will only escalate a situation. Be sure to stay in a visible public area; do not move to an enclosed area as the patron may follow you. Instead, move to an area with a physical barrier between you and the patron (e.g., a desk or counter) and where there are other coworkers.

Sample Scenario

A patron who has been wandering through the library, speaking to an invisible companion, approaches a staff person.

PATRON: That man is messing with my head.

STAFF: I'm sorry. I didn't understand you. Is someone bothering you?

PATRON: That man behind the tree is messing with my head. Tell him to leave me alone!

STAFF: I would be happy to help you with any questions you have about the library.

PATRON [*now visibly upset, voice raised*]: Tell that man behind the tree to leave me alone!

STAFF: Please lower your voice so I can help you. Were you looking for a book or magazine today?

EXERCISE

Patron Who Is Mentally Ill or under the Influence

Try scripting a scenario from your library:

PATRON:

STAFF:

PATRON:

STAFF:

PATRON:

STAFF:

PATRON:

STAFF:

PATRON:

STAFF:

PATRON:

STAFF:

Telephone and Virtual Encounters

The Bad News

Telephone and virtual encounters with angry patrons are especially difficult because you cannot rely on nonverbal cues. You cannot use your own body language to establish a comfortable climate, and you cannot use the patron's body language as clues to the direction to take. Be aware that your words and your paralanguage are more important than ever during telephone calls. Social scientists claim that tone of voice, pitch, and speed of speech account for 85 percent of communication over the phone. You don't even have paralanguage to rely on during virtual reference service (VRS) and communication by e-mail, text, or instant message.

The Good News

Telephone conversations and virtual exchange are often shorter than face-to-face discussions. And many staff find it easier to be assertive and firm in those situations than in person.

When talking with an angry patron on the telephone, follow the basic strategies as if he or she were physically present. In addition, try to:

- Answer the phone **by the third ring**. If you can't, apologize for the delay.

- **Set the tone** for the exchange. The patron makes a decision about you—and about the library—in the first five seconds.

- **Avoid a terse "please hold,"** which can exacerbate the caller's frustration.

- Talk **to** the person, **not at** her or him.

- Put the **smile** on your face into your voice. Studies have shown that we can often tell the expression on a caller's face over the telephone. It is easy to be deluded into thinking, "He can't see me rolling my eyes and clenching my fists," but the caller may still pick up on your hidden behavior from your paralanguage. (See Chapter 2 for more on paralanguage.)

- **Speak slightly slower** than usual. Because the patron cannot see you—and use your body language for clues and context—he or she may need longer to understand your words. However, do not speak so slowly that you sound condescending.

- If you have a high voice, **speak at the low end of your register**. The telephone accentuates high-pitched voices, making them sound screechy.

- Hold the receiver **one inch** from your mouth. Holding it closer can cause your words to sound slurred and/or to sound like you're shouting.

- **Listen carefully.** If he or she is repetitive or nervous, perhaps you are not listening well; these are typical behaviors of someone trying to get your attention. Remember to use "Hmm" or "I see" to let the caller know you are listening.

- **Avoid transferring the patron** because it seems as if you're avoiding the person. If you must transfer the call, be sure that the third party is available. Stay on the line until the proper party is found.

> Most people listen at only 10 percent efficiency on the telephone (as compared to 25 percent face-to-face). This means that after listening for ten minutes on the phone, the average person remembers only 10 percent of the discussion correctly.

- If you must put the person on hold—to get information or to calm down—do not leave him or her on hold for longer than 60 seconds (the telephone company says 30 seconds) without giving a progress report. Always **thank the person for waiting and apologize for any delays.**

- If you are unable to take the time necessary to handle the patron's request, make an appointment to call back at a more suitable time. Be sure that the caller understands why you must call back and agrees to the scheduled time. Then **call back** promptly and thank the person for waiting.

- **Allow the patron to hang up first.**

Unfortunately, many people feel that they can be rude on the telephone because they remain anonymous. Others feel that since you can't see them, it is somehow permissible to act out. We do not have statistics on the number of people who are rude over the phone. We do know that rude behavior in virtual users is rare; see Chapter 6 for more about this.

If a patron behaves unacceptably on the phone or in a one-on-one virtual setting (e.g., virtual reference service in e-mail, live chat, instant messaging, or text messaging), you should react much as you would in the parallel situation in person. That is, give the patron two opportunities to correct the behavior, explain why the behavior interferes with what he or she wants, and, if the behavior does not improve, assertively and calmly discontinue the exchange. (In public virtual settings, such as blogs or using social media networks, you must handle the situation differently. See Chapter 6 on this.)

Telephone

If a caller *screams* at you on the phone, ask him or her, "Please lower your voice. Yelling on the phone makes it hard to understand what you would like me to do." If the person continues, give a second warning by saying, "Please stop yelling. I cannot help you if you yell." If the person still screams, discontinue the call by saying, "I'm sorry. I cannot help you if you yell. Please call back when we can have a calmer conversation." Then hang up. An alternative script, if you know the patron's name and number—and if your supervisor agrees—is, "I'm sorry. I cannot deal with your yelling. I am going to have my supervisor call you back." Then hang up.

If a caller *curses* at you on the telephone, try this: "I really want to help you, but I'm having trouble with the language you're using. Would you please refrain from using that kind of language?" Most people will apologize and clean up their language. If not, give a second warning by saying, "I'm having trouble focusing on your question (request, complaint, etc.) because of the language you are using. Please stop."

If the patron continues to curse, discontinue the call by saying, "I'm sorry. I cannot help you. Please call back when we can have a more civil conversation." Then hang up. An alternative script, if you know the patron's name and number—and if your supervisor agrees—is, "I'm

When unhappy, the average customer remembers it for 23.5 months. When satisfied, the average customer remembers it for 18 months.

sorry. I cannot deal with this language. I am going to have my supervisor call you back." Then hang up.

If a caller *threatens* you physically, say, "I will not listen to this; I am going to hang up now" or "I can't help you. I will ask my supervisor to call you back." Then hang up and speak to your supervisor immediately. In some situations the supervisor may decide to call the telephone company or the police.

Virtual Encounters

In a text-based environment such as virtual reference service, the computer keyboard provides nonverbal cues which can be very helpful. Users employ emoticons, punctuation, and alphanumeric shortcuts to transmit feelings alongside the meaning expressed in words. It's important to maintain "word contact," the virtual equivalent of "eye contact," by typing short sentences and sending prompts frequently. Avoid typing in all caps ("shouting"), which is considered rude. (See Chapter 6 for more on virtual encounters.)

When a user is *impatient or angry*, be sure to remain polite; don't mirror rude behavior. You can ignore most rude behavior, but you may type "pds," which stands for "Please don't shout." Always show respect for the user's time. If he or she is angry about being on a waiting list or because of time lags between your replies, respond by typing, "I'm sorry you had to wait, but I can give you my full attention now."

If the patron continues to be angry or rude, ask him or her directly to stop. If he or she doesn't comply, suggest that the conversation be postponed until the patron can be civil. If that idea isn't acceptable and the rude behavior continues, tell that patron that you will log off and then do so immediately.

If the patron *curses* at you or uses unacceptable language, respond by typing, "Please refrain from that kind of language." If the patron persists, type something like, "If you do not change your language, I will log off." If that doesn't work, type, "I am logging off now. Please try our service again when you can use polite language." And then log off.

QUICK REVIEW

Handling Difficult Situations

- Treat complaints as an opportunity to please one patron and a chance to improve your service to many others.
- When faced with a complaint, listen, sympathize, and apologize before restating the problem and offering alternative solutions.
- If a patron accuses you or a colleague, translate the comment into a request for a service that you can provide.
- Never get pulled into a discussion of an accusation, and don't ask questions about it.
- Do not respond reflexively to an accusation or repeat the negative label.
- A fine line exists between angry encounters and unacceptable confrontations. The difference is in the behavior.
- When a patron is using unacceptable behavior, be sure to label and disapprove of the behavior only.
- Stress how the unacceptable behavior causes a response that is counterproductive for the patron and work toward a solution.
- If a patron will not discontinue the unacceptable behavior, be clear and assertive as you ask him or her to leave the library.
- With a mentally ill patron or a person under the influence, it is essential to project a sense of calm and keep a wide comfort zone for the patron. Involve another staff person if possible, and walk away if you feel you are in danger.
- Coping with an angry patron over the telephone or in a virtual environment is especially difficult because you don't have nonverbal cues to help you understand the patron and you cannot use body language to communicate.
- On the phone, speak to the person slightly more slowly than usual and at the low end of your vocal register.
- Avoid transferring angry patrons or putting them on hold.
- If necessary, after giving two warnings, tell the patron that you are going to hang up and do so.
- In a virtual setting, keep in "word contact" by typing short replies and sending prompts frequently.
- Don't use all caps (which is considered shouting), and don't allow the patron to use them either.
- If necessary, after giving two warnings, tell the patron that you are logging off and do so.

The Digital Landscape

Our electronic age presents increased opportunities for angry people to vent their displeasure. Most libraries have webpages and blogs, and most offer some virtual reference services (VRS). These include synchronous approaches such as live chat, videoconferencing, cobrowsing, and VoIP (voice-over Internet protocol). Asynchronous VRS include instant messaging and text messaging, e-mail, blogs, wikis, and the virtual reference desk in Second Life.

Psychologists report that conflict can be heightened online by what is called the "disinhibition effect." John Suler (2002), an expert in the area, explains that cyberspace encourages "rude language, harsh criticisms, anger, hatred and even threats." He believes that the disinhibition effect is caused or heightened by the following features of online communication: anonymity, invisibility, delayed reactions, the perception that the interaction is in your head, and the neutralizing of status.

These same features make anger on the Internet especially difficult to handle. In addition, we do not have visual cues and body language to help us understand what is happening, and we also cannot take advantage of auditory cues (paralanguage, including voice, pitch, and speed of speech). Worst of all, in the case of social media, one patron's anger can evolve quickly into an extremely public confrontation.

As in the in-person, on-the-ground, analog real world, the solution is a combination of good customer service attitudes, strong communication skills, prudent policies, and thoughtful procedures.

Virtual Reference Service

Fortunately, a national study reports that, despite fears that the anonymous nature of VRS would allow users to act out, analysis of transcripts has found otherwise. Marie Radford and her colleagues (2010) report that only a small minority of users are impatient or rude: 10 percent were impatient and 4 percent made rude or insulting remarks. Only 2 percent used profanity or inappropriate language. Interestingly, approximately 33

Defusing the Angry Patron

A growing base of research confirms that users in virtual settings highly value the relationship dimension, along with content and information delivery, in their perception of success.
—Marie Radford

percent showed rapid disconnect by users—usually a display of frustration or anger—often after the librarian rudely implied that the user was wasting his or her time (e.g., asking if the user had already checked the database).

As to be expected, the research found that the same interactions that anger users in a face-to-face (FtF) setting also irritate them in VRS. Two of the most common irritants are unmonitored referrals (sending patrons to a resource without checking back that they were able to find or use it) and negative closures (behaviors to get rid of a patron prematurely). Others are implying that the user should have looked harder before requesting assistance, claiming that the information is not available or doesn't exist, ignoring cues that the user wants more help, being judgmental of the subject matter, sending the patron somewhere else, and offering assistance that never materializes.

The Reference and User Services Association (RUSA) of the American Library Association has published "Guidelines for Implementing and Maintaining Virtual Reference Services." These state:

> Virtual reference requires of library staff many of the same communication and interpersonal skills necessary for other forms of reference. The absence of a physically present patron and the different modes of communication may call for additional skills, effort or training to provide quality service on par to face-to-face reference services.

The guidelines refer the reader to the ALA "Guidelines for Behavioral Performance of Reference and Information Service Providers," which were discussed in Chapter 2. Librarians have found that courtesy, friendliness, and the best practices in FtF settings are equally helpful in digital environments. Some of these are greeting the user, showing respect for the user's time, offering alternatives, being empathetic, and building rapport.

As mentioned in Chapter 5, in the text-based environment the computer keyboard provides nonverbal cues for building a relationship. Experts suggest using alphanumeric shortcuts (such as typing "4U" instead of "for you"), asterisks or other punctuation for emphasis, and emoticons; and spelling out nonverbal behaviors (such as "ha ha"). It's important, too, to maintain "word contact," the virtual equivalent of eye contact. To keep the patron from waiting long between exchanges, type short sentences and send prompts frequently to convey interest (e.g., "I am looking at source now").

When people are frustrated or angry:

- Remain polite; don't mirror rude behavior.
- Don't admonish the user for most rude behavior (e.g., "flaming" or posting an angry message), though it's acceptable to type "pds" for "Please don't shout."
- Don't condescend to a person who has a basic question.
- Avoid typing in all caps ("shouting"), which is considered rude.
- Show respect for the user's time. For example, "I'm sorry you had to wait, but I can give you my full attention now."

- Tell an impatient user exactly how long you expect the interchange to take and offer options. For example, "This will take me 5 to 10 minutes. If you do not have time to wait now, I can e-mail the information for you to pull up later."

Websites and Social Media

In the 1990s, the traditional comment box evolved, in many libraries, into a public bulletin board with user complaints or suggestions and staff responses. Now, in the digital age, patron opinions are more public than we ever imagined possible—seen by hundreds or thousands of people reading the library's website or Facebook page—or an upset patron's blog or tweet. Even worse, an angry user can post a complaint online, and it can spread virally by appearing in search engine results. As Pete Blackshaw writes in his book *Satisfied Customers Tell Three Friends: Angry Customers Tell 3,000*, "blog postings, message boards, websites aren't like graffiti which can be painted over or washed away. Instead they [leave] indelible tracks...that sustain negative impressions for excruciatingly long periods of time."

It is extremely difficult to define the line between freedom of speech and unacceptable behavior on the web. When is it appropriate to delete comments, to report posters to an Internet service provider, or to block people from a social networking community? Bloggers who work in the nonprofit sphere are urgently discussing strategies for handling social media. They note that users (or "fans") want the site editor (i.e., the library) to block abusive and angry posts before they upset other users, who may then disengage from the page and the services offered by the site owner. Detailed directions on how to block people from Facebook, Twitter, MySpace, YouTube, Flickr, and individual blogs, as well as how to collapse threads and restrict your wall on Facebook, are widely available. A psychiatrist who moderates an online support group has even developed an intricate formula for sentencing posters who are repeatedly uncivil, taking into account whether the person has been blocked before, is uncivil in more than one way, in more than one post, multiple times in a single post, etc. He reports that all of this is complicated by the fact that a person who is blocked can still read what others post and can try to post under another name.

News sites, including those developed by mainstream commercial newspapers, are still experimenting with ways to improve and expand online discussion by readers while reducing the quantity of inflammatory comments. The *Wall Street Journal* has required commenters to register and provide their real names since 2008, and other newspaper sites are considering doing that. According to a recent article on CNN.com, many site editors feel that anonymity is the root cause of irresponsible and uncivil comments; they are moving away from anonymous comments and requiring registration with real names or at least a valid e-mail address and user name. Others disagree. An editor of the website of the nonprofit school for journalists, Poynter.org, states that the website

> It is the triumph of reason to get on well with those who possess none.
> —Voltaire

owner must clearly and repeatedly advise readers of what sort of responses the site wants as well as the site's commenting guidelines. Arianna Huffington, cofounder and editor of *The Huffington Post*, still gives posters the opportunity to comment anonymously but has initiated a system to involve more of the "HuffPost community" in the comment moderation process. The system also awards commenters who post regularly and who flag inappropriate comments. She feels that rewarding active, insightful commenters will lead to fewer nasty, hateful commenters.

Librarians, too, are struggling with controlling angry comments on social media while at the same time encouraging more robust and civil activity. A recent article (Porter and King, 2009) about ugly posts on a public library website stresses that libraries need to respond quickly by using all available web tools. That doesn't necessarily mean deleting angry or objectionable posts, though, "because the library is in complete control . . . staff can easily correct misinformation or point to the correct answer."

The consensus seems to be that although we have no control over what people post on their own blogs, social networking sites, or even in print newspapers, policies and procedures can protect the library from rants on its pages—much the way they control patron behavior in person in the analog world. Libraries should:

- Consider prohibiting anonymous comments and requiring all posters to register and/or use a real name.

- Designate staff moderators who will monitor each website, blog, or public page numerous times each day, responding to questions and correcting misinformation or apologizing when appropriate. It's essential to respond immediately.

- Decide that all comments added to the library website or blog should be moderated (i.e., e-mailed to a designated staff member, rather than being published automatically). After reviewing the comment, staff can decide whether to post the comment and how to respond. Again, responses must be timely in this fast-paced environment.

- Encourage comments and stress that posters can disagree or argue as long as they remain civil.

- Create and post community guidelines of acceptable behavior on all blogs and webpages. For example, ask people to stick to the topic being discussed, to avoid posting spam, and to be polite in their posts.

- Refer to the guidelines often, especially when a rude comment is posted.

- Intervene immediately when commenters are not civil to one another or about the library.

- Be prepared to join a comment thread or forum to refocus discussion as needed.

- Ask your readers to contact the site administrator if they notice rude or abusive posts.

- Delete comments only in extreme situations.

- Block posters only after repeat offenses and warnings.

Meanwhile, a new, related, and disturbing problem with social networking sites has arisen: library staff flaming, gossiping, or complaining about customers. Could the disinhibition effect apply to library staff? Although venting may be acceptable face-to-face with trusted colleagues, complaining online is not. As one library blogger posted recently, "There's an argument that it's ok if you have a private feed. Let me assure you that nothing is ever private. It only takes one person who you previously trusted to press 'print screen' and then paste that screen shot into an email to your manager to let you know that there is no such thing as privacy." In addition, the rude comments can easily spill over onto public sites because the web is so densely interlinked.

For example, a Twitter feed may be set up to flow into a Facebook feed. Or, as another library blogger asked, "What happens when the patron who was complained about on Twitter decides to use Twitter, wants to connect with people...so he/she does that 'find everyone within 20 miles of this zip code' search, and discovers the librarian virtually hollering at him/her?" And what if a search engine points to the complaint on its search results pages? Clearly this is an area which begs for more open discussion among all who work in libraries and which requires stricter guidelines.

> Expressing anger is a form of public littering.
> —Willard Gaylin

QUICK REVIEW

Navigating the Digital Landscape

- Virtual reference services require similar interpersonal and communication skills as in-person and telephone services.
- Displaying courtesy and empathy in your choice of words is even more important in the virtual sphere because neither you nor the user has visual or auditory cues on which to rely.
- Computer keystrokes can serve as nonverbal cues in establishing rapport with the patron.
- Remember to maintain "word contact."
- Remain polite even if the user is rude.
- Always inform the patron how long you expect the interchange to take.
- Post behavior guidelines on the library website, blog, and public page.
- Appoint a moderator to check posts regularly and to intervene as necessary.
- Consider eliminating anonymous postings.
- Balance the needs for freedom of speech and library openness with the need to preserve civility and the library's reputation.
- Develop guidelines for staff postings about the library on public sites.

Coping with Your Own Anger

How often have you thought "How dare he talk to me like that?" while an angry person is venting at you? Even when we know that we should not take the tirade personally—that we should separate ourselves as individuals from our roles as library staff—we still think "Why me?" and "Who do you think you are?" Often people facing angry customers become angry themselves, as though anger is contagious. It is extremely difficult to stay calm during an angry encounter, and even staffers who can do that often feel angry afterward.

It may be hard to believe, but angry people do not store up their frustrations to dump them all at the library. Anyone working directly with customers faces the problem of secondhand anger. The *Wall Street Journal* reports, "[C]ustomer service workers face more frequent personal attacks than people in most other occupations, with little or no opportunity to respond. . . . As a group, customer service people are more prone to illness, absenteeism, stress-related disability claims and family leave requests" (Shellenbarger, 2004). The key phrase here is "with little or no opportunity to respond."

Psychologists agree that it is unhealthy to deny anger or to store it up. Holding onto anger can lead to sleep disorders, chronic anxiety, and high blood pressure, among other things. However, blowing off steam is counterproductive. The National Institute for Mental Health reports, "People who have skills at managing their anger are less likely to suffer from emotional disorders or to be early victims of heart disease or stroke." So the question is how to manage (or release) the anger in a healthy manner.

During the Encounter

First of all, **breathe**. Although this sounds like foolish advice—you've probably never stopped breathing—slow, deep breathing is an excellent relaxant. Breathe in through your nose to the count of five, expanding your diaphragm as you inhale. Then breathe out through your mouth to

> For every minute you remain angry, you give up sixty seconds of peace of mind.
>
> —Ralph Waldo Emerson

> Holding onto anger is like grasping a hot coal with the intent of throwing it at someone else; you are the one who gets burned.
>
> —Buddha

the count of five, contracting your diaphragm as you exhale. Be sure to breathe deeply and from the diaphragm. If you're not sure how to do this, lie down and place your fingers on your rib cage. When lying down, we breathe from the diaphragm naturally. Note how your fingers move out on inhalation and in on exhalation. Now try it again, standing up. It may help to picture your breath coming up from your gut and then out your mouth. Diaphragmatic breathing may seem artificial at first, but it is key for athletes, singers, and actors, as well as for people releasing anger. This technique can be done anywhere; it is invisible to others.

Observe the cues your body is giving you. The trick here is to catch yourself before you become really angry or upset. For example, if your thoughts are indignant or you have a desire to fight back, stop yourself. Likewise, take note if you have physical indicators of anger, such as tense muscles, rapid heartbeat, or clenched teeth.

Use self-talk or internal monologue to keep your anger from escalating and to take charge of your emotions. You might silently say to yourself, "I am not going to get angry. I will stay in control" or "I will not take this personally. I can better help the patron and myself if I stay calm" or "This will pass. I can do this" or "Take it easy."

Monitor the cues you are giving to others. Imagine that you are looking in a mirror. What is your facial expression? What is your body language? Are you showing any frustration or anger? If so, you may be escalating the situation. Control your breathing and your facial expression to change the signals you are giving—and meanwhile you will calm yourself. For example, consciously altering your expression by unwrinkling your brow will meanwhile relax your forehead.

Change your physical position in your chair or sit down if you have been standing. If you are leaning far forward (which is a fighting posture), lean back partway instead. If you are leaning all the way back (which can look like you're avoiding the interchange), lean partly forward (a listening posture). Adjust your posture by placing your open hands at your sides. Drop your shoulders. When stressed, most people raise their shoulders, which limits circulation to the brain. By lowering your shoulders, you restore the flow of oxygen and blood to the brain so you can feel calmer and think more clearly.

Watch your paralanguage. Are you speaking in a higher pitch or volume than usual? Are you speaking more quickly than usual? Focus on keeping your voice calm and on speaking slowly, quietly, and carefully. Often lowering your voice will calm both you and the patron.

Try a **muscle relaxation** exercise. Ironically, the simplest way to relax muscles is to tense them first. Using your toes (since they are out of sight of the patron), tense your muscles by curling your toes as tightly as possible for a count of five and then relax them. If you can do it unobtrusively, do the same with your fingers.

Focus on the situation rather than the emotion, and on the patron rather than yourself. Direct all your energy toward solutions. Ask yourself, "How can I move us toward a solution to end this negative encounter as quickly and effectively as possible?" Concentrate on what to do—and what you want to achieve—instead of on the patron's anger.

> I don't have to attend every argument I'm invited to.
> —Anonymous

Avoid "blind rage." Any intense emotional experience—like coping with an angry patron—can blind you. In this context, Gentry (2007), an anger management expert, explains,

> blind simply means your brain is not paying any attention to anything outside your own emotion. The good news, however, is that the brain can be distracted—meaning it can turn its attention elsewhere at any point in time. So the trick . . . is to give your brain something else to attend to besides anger.

Immediately Afterward

Drink cold water. It will cool you down and force you to breathe more slowly. Avoid drinks with caffeine or excess sugar, though, as they are stimulants.

Give yourself a **ten-second massage**. Rub your stiff neck, sore shoulder, or aching head for ten or fifteen seconds for some instant relief.

Suck on a hard candy until it's all gone. Gentry (2007) suggests:

> It only takes five minutes, but it short-circuits the natural progression of anger. . . . Sweet sensations are associated at the level of the brain with pleasure which is the antithesis of anger. . . . [Also] by putting something in your mouth to suck on, you can't immediately verbalize your anger.

Don't inflate the significance of the situation. Gentry (2007) notes:

> When you continue to rethink, reconsider, relive and rehash some incident that provoked your anger well beyond the point where it happened, you're ruminating. And rumination invariably intensifies emotions . . . . [W]hen you become aware that you are entering into the realm of repetitive angry thinking, say aloud to yourself "Stop!" and shift your attention to something else. Repeat the word as many times as necessary until you have let go of what's irritating you.

It may help you to **reframe your perception** of what happened. In other words, rationalize the user's behavior by offering yourself a different explanation of the incident. Can you think of reasons—health problems, pressure at work or school, family issues—to explain the person's angry behavior? "Whatever the reason, try to understand the person or give him an excuse to be upset. By trying to be understanding of the person's behavior, your frustration may be decreased" (Fescemyer, 2002).

Another way to reconsider what you've been through is to consider the ways in which handling angry people can be beneficial to you. This is the silver lining approach to life. Remind yourself that you are learning to think on your feet and under pressure. You are increasing your tolerance for others, your empathy, and your patience.

A popular **stress management** technique is to imagine a large balloon over your head, filled with all your unused expletives, unspoken insults, grumpy thoughts, and your vengeful or hurt feelings. Then imagine the

So you think you can't change? Every five days you get a new stomach lining. Every month you get new skin. And you replace 98 percent of all the atoms in your body in less than a year.

balloon floating away—or being popped—so everything in the balloon is gone. A variation on this is to write down all the negative thoughts and emotions on a piece of paper. Then burn the paper, destroying it and your negativity.

Try **muscle relaxation** again, this time using the whole body. Starting with the toes and, working up the body, tense your muscles for a count of five and then relax them. For example, curl your toes as tight as possible for the count of five and then stretch them back out. Or stand up and drill your toes into the floor. Then tighten the rest of the body in this order: calves, thighs, and hips; fingers, arms, chest, and stomach; head, forehead, and neck. Your whole body should shake from tension as you raise your arms over your head and stretch as far as you can. Finally, tense and release all your muscles at the same time and feel a warmth flow through your body. The whole exercise takes only five minutes and leaves you feeling renewed. Not only is your body relaxed, but your mind is also. A great paradox of life is that although your mind caused the body to tense, you can use your body to calm the mind.

In *Controlling the Confrontation*, Lustberg recommends another muscle relaxation method. In this one, you tense and relax your neck and head muscles. Draw your neck taut until you feel your vertical muscle and vein lines. Purse your lips and draw your jaw as tight as possible while clenching your teeth. Tighten your forehead until your eyes are barely open. Your entire head should shake. Now relax.

Rigorous exercise reduces anger and stress. Even a quick walk around the block or a series of sit-ups in the staff room can soothe body and mind. After work, any regular physical exercise—swimming, jogging, dancing—can be a stress reducer. **Nonstrenuous slow exercises** like yoga can relax your muscles and calm you, too.

Another technique to try is **visual imagery**. For this you need a quiet, private place for a few minutes. Sitting or lying down, close your eyes and breathe deeply. Then imagine yourself in a scene of perfect tranquility—perhaps a beautiful and serene landscape or a favorite place from a happy time in your own life. Hold the pleasant feelings when you open your eyes and go back to work.

Laughter is a great antidote to anger. Reread a favorite book of humor, look at those comic strip clippings by your desk, or watch a movie that always makes you laugh. Laugh at yourself, too, by refusing to take yourself too seriously. The American Psychological Association recommends,

> When you catch yourself feeling [that you should not have to tolerate the unbearable indignity of anything that keeps you from having your way], picture yourself as a God or Goddess, a supreme ruler who owns the streets and stores and office space, striding alone, and having your way in all situations while others defer to you. The more detail you can get into your imaginary scenes, the more chance you have to realize that maybe you are being a little unreasonable. And using silly humor can make you laugh at yourself, and lose your anger. (Spielberger and Deffenbacher, n.d.)

> I know of no more disagreeable situation than to be left feeling generally angry without anybody in particular to be angry at.
> —Frank Moore Colby

Later

Talk it out with your buddy, if you have one, or with a colleague or friend. (See more on buddies in Strategy 25 in Chapter 3.) Getting it off your chest can be a literal relief. First, express your emotions by using statements that begin with "I feel..." Next, ask how the other person would have felt in the situation; usually this helps you to see that you are not alone in your feelings. Finally, use this as an opportunity to get a new perspective, which might help you next time by discussing the situation rather than the emotions. Describe what happened and ask what your friend or colleague would have done instead.

Request a **debriefing meeting**. Gathering the staff for such a meeting provides a safe and constructive outlet for you as well as a chance for your coworkers to learn from your experience. It also gives your supervisor a chance to congratulate you and others on their good work.

> He who angers you conquers you.
> —Elizabeth Kenny

Ongoing

Do you use a lot of blaming statements about others or "should" statements about yourself? These are often indicators of unrealistically high expectations. **Counteract unrealistic expectations** of others and of yourself by identifying them. For example, "People (or I) should know better than that" or "Things need to go a certain way; anything else is wrong" or "How can he or she think that?" In fact, it is okay for people to feel and think differently from the way we do. And it is okay if things happen in a way that we have not chosen.

High self-expectations and a need for perfection can lead to much guilt and anger. People who often tell themselves "I should have done that" or "I shouldn't have said that" create anger for themselves. Similarly, people who feel they must always be in control or must never disappoint others often feel that they are failures after an angry episode—their own or a patron's.

Keeping a journal about the occasions of anger may be helpful. Medical research has shown that writing about traumatic experiences measurably improves the health of some medical patients. In one study, people in the treatment group were instructed to write their deepest thoughts and feelings while members of the control group wrote about their plans for the day. Only the participants in the first group experienced positive results. The researchers suspect that "the writing task may be effective because it allows people to synthesize and make sense of their experience...to alter the way they think about an event, giving it order and structure." The writing measurably improved the health of patients with chronic asthma or rheumatoid arthritis—certainly it should help with stress caused by angry library patrons!

Writing is one way you can help **change self-damaging thought patterns**. Are there certain words or behaviors that trigger your anger? Do you have irrational thought patterns? Once you understand what provokes you, you can take steps to change those thoughts. Because

Defusing the Angry Patron

thinking precedes feelings, you can change your feelings, which in turn will affect your behavior.

Psychologist Albert Ellis's (2003) pioneering work on anger outlined a series of irrational thoughts that can lead to anger. His sequence is: "I want something (e.g., to be treated with respect). I didn't get it. It is awful and terrible not to get what I want. You shouldn't frustrate me! You're bad for frustrating me. Bad people ought to be punished." Does this model ring true?

Other forms of negative thinking that can lead to anger include:

- Blaming others (or yourself), which reflects a need for control—including placing responsibility on someone.

- Exaggerating the importance of problems or dwelling on the negative. Instead, we can remind ourselves that what happened may be frustrating, but it's not the end of the world; getting angry or negative won't help.

- Minimizing or discounting the positive, including not giving yourself credit when you do things well.

- Labeling people (including yourself) instead of their behavior.

- Seeing issues as black and white, and situations as all or nothing. This includes using "never" and "always" in your self-talk or in talking with others. These words may justify your anger, but they work against problem solving. They may also discourage others from collaborating with you on finding solutions.

- Predicting the outcome as negative by interpreting signs pessimistically; this can become a self-fulfilling prophecy.

- Using overdramatic words and exaggerations when talking to yourself while you are angry.

Moderate exercise (e.g., riding a stationary bike for 30 minutes) reduces your capacity to become angry. Recent research has shown that "exercise, even a single bout of it, can have a robust prophylactic effect" on anger, according to Nathaniel Thom (2010), a stress physiologist and the lead researcher on a recent study. Students, selected for their "short fuses," were shown slides designed to induce anger. The students who had exercised did not become as angry as those who had not exercised. Exercise didn't inure them to what they saw, but it kept their anger from escalating. We still don't know how exercise blunts anger, but scientists theorize that serotonin (a neurotransmitter in the brain) is the key. "Animal studies have found that low levels of serotonin are associated with aggression which is our closest analogue to anger," Thom reports. "Exercise increases serotonin levels in the rat brain."

Reward yourself for your successes. When you are able to manage your anger, give yourself a reward. Rewards not only recognize positive steps but also help people make further progress. Be sure the reward is one that is relaxing and pleasurable. To increase the enjoyment, decide in advance what you'd like to do for yourself, write it down, and make yourself a promise. To use the future reward as a tool to handle a difficult encounter, focus on the reward whenever you are tempted to get pulled in.

Reconsider your model of anger to affect your future encounters with angry people. Most of us subscribe to a model that involves direct stimulus and effect: Something is said or done that causes the anger. But many psychologists feel that we have a choice of whether to become angry. In other words, the same words or actions that could lead to anger do not have to make us irate. In this model, we can choose whether to react with anger. We have the ability to take a proactive, thoughtful course and choose anger only if it is useful to us. For example, if a patron's behavior is threatening, anger may alert us to danger and energize us to respond. But our anger is not useful if a patron vents his frustration that his time on the Internet is up; reacting with anger will not help us—or him—in this situation. In fact, anger will only cause us harm by increasing our stress and giving a negative impression of the library.

In this model, a reflexive or reactive response of anger is considered a learned response. So, we can learn to respond differently with time and practice. For example, we can teach ourselves new ways of responding by reminding ourselves, "This is frustrating, but it's not the end of the world, and getting angry won't fix it anyway." A more systemic way to change our responses is to recognize how situations in the past have conditioned our current response patterns and to release those parts of the past we'd like to put behind us. Practitioners of this approach believe that freedom from the past means no longer being dominated by its influences. And that greater self-awareness leads to healthier ways of living in the present.

The Bottom Line

What is the one constant in every exchange you have with an angry patron? You. We may not be able to change all the library's stress points or all the users' behaviors, but we can work to change our own responses. The only real control we have is self-control.

> To rule one's anger is well; to prevent it is still better.
>
> —Tyron Edwards

> Use cold hard logic on yourself. Logic defeats anger, because anger, even when justified, can quickly become irrational.
>
> —Spielberger and Deffenbacher

QUICK REVIEW

Coping with Your Anger

- Don't take the patron's anger personally.
- Focus on the situation rather than on the patron or yourself.
- During the encounter, remember to breathe slowly and monitor your body language and paralanguage.
- Use self-talk or internal monologue to take charge of your emotions.
- Change your sitting or standing position, and try muscle relaxation techniques during an angry interchange.
- Immediately after an angry exchange, drink cold water, suck on a hard candy, and/or do more muscle relaxation exercises.
- Don't escalate your anger, and consider reframing your perception of what happened.
- Later, talk to your buddy and hold a debriefing meeting with other staff members.
- Imagery, journal writing, exercise, and laughter can help after an angry encounter.
- For a long-term approach to managing your own anger, change negative thought patterns and counteract unrealistic expectations of yourself.
- Reward yourself for managing your anger.
- Reconsider your model of anger.
- Remember that the only control we have is self-control.

Help Is at Hand

All library staff members who work with the public should learn about the tools available to them for defusing an angry patron. This chapter presents six of these tools, all of which deserve attention before any encounters with customers, although one will be not be used until after an angry interaction.

The library's policies and regulations, which determine how the library does its work and how patrons are treated, combine to form the first and most important of the tools. It's important that all library staffers understand all of the policies in the context of the library's mission and philosophy. But it is *essential* that staffers know the policies and procedures on coping with angry patrons and other difficult situations.

Policies and Procedures

Policies

A library's policies and regulations should be a strong structure to prevent patron anger and support library staff. Instead, they often are a source of frustration for both users and staff. (Review the related exercise in Chapter 2.) Policies should reflect the library's values and mission. If a policy conflicts with the library's philosophy or goals, it is difficult for staff to implement. The library's mission statement should serve as a preamble to all policies so that the relationship between mission and policy is clear. For instance, if a library is committed to being a resource for everyone in the community, the library's policy on library cards should enable the maximum number of people to obtain a card by making it easy to get one with a minimum of paperwork.

The library's policies on patron behavior and security are the most germane to our topic. A 2008 study of public library security by the Ohio Library Council found that 91 percent (of the 98 respondents) had security policies. Although there is no comparable national study, an educated guess is that most public and academic libraries in the United States have policies about patron behavior.

IN THIS CHAPTER:

✔ Policies and Procedures

✔ Stress Point Identification

✔ Rebuttal Files

✔ Quick Reference Guides

✔ Incident Reports

✔ Security and Other Staff

> All things are difficult before they are easy.
>
> —Thomas Fuller

Defusing the Angry Patron

As anyone who provides direct customer service knows, sometimes upholding policy is unpopular with patrons. Although the public library is a public facility, access to it is a "limited right," so the library retains the right to define its public and delineate the services available. For example, many public libraries provide different services and charge different fees for nonresidents versus residents. Similarly, an academic library defines whom it will serve and with which specific services. However, most people assume that if they are allowed in the door, they have the right to service. Because of that misunderstanding, academic libraries should have two official policies: one on admission and another on services.

Looking at the current rules of conduct of many public and academic libraries, it is clear that two changes in the makeup of library users have affected how behavior policies are written. First, because library users reflect the changing demographics of our communities, libraries serve a very diverse group of people, many of whom come from cultures without public libraries and may not know how they are expected to behave. Second, because library materials have become available in many more formats, libraries are serving more people who are not traditional library users. For example, libraries serve people in a wider range of ages, with more types of disabilities, and some who use the library remotely. The result of these changes is that libraries have learned that their policies must be available in multiple languages and formats and must use language that is clear and explicit.

In addition, library behavior policies must be specific and based in law because of recent lawsuits which have defined a library's rights to limit user behaviors. Mary Minow (2009), a library law expert, explained one important 2003 case (*Neinast v. Board of Trustees*):

> The U.S. Court of Appeals for the 3d and 6th Circuits held that a library is a limited public forum insofar as the library must permit the public to exercise the right to receive information and ideas consistent with the nature of the library as a place for reading, writing and quiet contemplation.

In other words, a library has the right to enforce reasonable rules of conduct in keeping with its mission as long as it also protects the rights of the public to use the library. Other courts have held that in order to be legally valid, conduct policies must be written narrowly about specific behaviors and must target behavior rather than class or status of people.

Minow (2009) offers the mnemonic device FEND to remind libraries how to fend off lawsuits about their behavior codes: **F**irst Amendment, **E**qual Enforcement, **N**otice, and **D**ue Process.

- The **First Amendment** defines freedom of speech; libraries cannot restrict what people say, only what they do. For example, using obnoxious language is not prohibited; it is protected by the First Amendment, so libraries may not ask people to leave only because of their choice of language. Libraries may, however, ask patrons to monitor their choice of words and to speak quietly.

If the language becomes threatening or harassing, it is no longer protected.

- **Equal Enforcement** means that any rule must be applied equally to all people; any decision about misuse of the library must be based on actual behavior and not upon distinctions among people or classes of people. The point is to have objective standards and fair enforcement. For example, a library cannot assume a patron will behave (or misbehave) a certain way because of his or her history. Also, a library cannot ask teens to use the computer stations one at a time if it allows customers of other ages to use them in groups. (Exceptions can be made for parents helping children under 12 and for people with disabilities.)

- **Notice** refers to people's right to know the library policies and regulations; the library must provide a clear description of the behaviors that are prohibited and the penalties that can be imposed. Behavior policies should be distributed to all patrons when they register for library cards and should be posted at each entrance to the library building and on the webpage. Similarly, patrons using library computers should be required to click on an "I accept the policies of this public library" button in order to access the catalog, databases, or the Internet. Patrons accept the rules of conduct if they have read them and then apply for a library card or sign up for use of a meeting room, or if they use any of the library's services in analog or digital form.

- **Due Process** means that people must have the right and ability to appeal any penalty. The policy must include a statement on the process for patrons to appeal to the library director and the library board, or some other authority above the director.

> Information is pretty thin unless mixed with experience.
> —Clarence Day

Because publicly expressed anger is so common these days, libraries are creating policies about angry, disruptive behavior along with policies on typical behavior issues such as cell phone use, leaving children unattended, and so forth.

The American Library Association's "Guidelines for the Development of Policies and Procedures Regarding User Behavior and Library Usage" offers excellent guidance on writing rules for behavior. It stresses that libraries need to protect the patron's right to access unless there's a compelling reason to deny it. "Policies and regulations that impose restrictions on library access should apply only to those activities that materially interfere with the public's right of access to library facilities, the safety of users and staff, and protection of library resources and facilities." In terms of angry patrons, two guidelines are especially relevant:

- "Policies should not be based upon an assumption or expectation that certain users might engage in behaviors that could disrupt library service...."

- "Policies should not restrict access to the library by persons who merely inspire the anger or annoyance of others. Policies based upon appearance or behavior that is merely annoying, or that merely generates negative subjective reactions from others, do not meet the necessary standard. Such policies should employ a reasonable, objective standard based on the behavior itself."

A conduct policy must describe the consequences for people who do not behave in accordance with the library regulations. Such penalties typically range from suspension of library services for a set period of time to notification of police to liability for damages to property, depending on the level of misbehavior. As mentioned previously, the policy must also describe an appeals process; typically the patron has the right to appeal to the library director and board of directors. The draft policy, including the penalties and appeals protocol, should be reviewed by the library's lawyers and by the appropriate police department to ensure that it's compatible with local laws. It's also wise to have the draft reviewed by a library board member and a representative community member to ensure that it's appropriate and understandable. Then the full library board must approve the policy.

Note that some experts advise staff to show angry patrons the relevant policy as a way of deflecting anger from the staff person; they believe that customers will become less upset if they are directed to the policy that shows they are not being treated unjustly. Others think the opposite is true—that angry patrons become more frustrated when faced with a policy. A way around this debate is to present the policy as a reflection of the users' wishes. For example, instead of saying "Our library policy bans cell phone use inside the building," you might say, "Users have asked us to restrict cell phone use in the library."

Procedures

No matter how well a policy is written and disseminated, it is useless without codified procedures for staff to enforce it. Although enforcement procedures were relatively rare in the past, more and more libraries are now creating procedures and training staff about them. The Ohio Library Council study previously mentioned found that 26 percent of the responding libraries had policies but no procedures.

Standardized procedures result in more consistent enforcement by staff across departments and branches; such uniformity is necessary to ensure fair enforcement. An accepted protocol also makes it easier for staff to uphold policies; instead of worrying about what is fair and what should be done in a given situation, staff members focus on carrying out the accepted procedures that they have been taught. Procedures for dangerous situations, for example, should include when to call the police, what to expect when the police arrive, when to call another agency (e.g., mental health services), and any legal responsibilities of staff. A list of emergency telephone numbers and a script for calling the police should also be included.

A procedures manual should be updated regularly and be readily available to all staff members, in print and/or in a file on the staff intranet. Some libraries, such as the Fresno (CA) Public Library, have an ongoing intranet-based discussion of the policies and procedures as related to problem situations that arise. All public service staff should be authorized and required to uphold the policies, and all supervisors and managers should support their staff in training and implementation of the procedures.

Mandatory staff training in library policies and procedures is imperative. Staff must know what to do, and all staff must apply the rules in the same way. Elizabeth Waller and Patricia Bangs of the Fairfax County (VA) Public Library report: "We measure the success of our *Problem Behavior Manual* by the comfort level of our staff and the consistency of their responses throughout our twenty-one branches."

Training should also focus on the "why" behind the policies and procedures, both in terms of the law and in consideration of the library's philosophy and mission statement. For example, the Salt Lake County (UT) Library has a "Library Customer Bill of Rights" which delineates the behaviors that users can expect from staff, such as "Customers will always be treated courteously, in all circumstances and at all times" and "Library customers' complaints/problems will be resolved in 48 hours whenever possible." The Salt Lake County (UT) Library also has a "Library Use and Behavior Policy," which lists ten regulations for patrons. Two of these are "Show courtesy and respect to other customers by using voice, behavior and personal hygiene that will not disturb others" and "Show courtesy and respect to library staff by complying with requests from staff." In staff training, employees are taught both the Bill of Rights and the Behavior Policy.

In a similar vein, the Fairfax County (VA) Public Library prefaces its *Problem Behavior Manual* with the following guiding principles:

- Every single customer who uses our libraries should feel welcomed, valued, and respected. We assume that everyone has a legitimate reason to use our facility.

- All of our rules are applied humanely, courteously, and fairly to all customers. We do not make assumptions about customers based on their physical appearance or any other characteristic.

- Every day is a new beginning, and we do not assume a problem will occur because of past experience.

- Every customer is entitled to their own style of using the public library, as long as it does not interfere with the rights of others.

- Not all odd behaviors are problem behaviors. Each situation must be judged on its own merits and against our definition of what constitutes a true problem.

- Once it has been determined that a problem does exist, library staff will be expected to take prompt, reasonable and appropriate action to resolve or eliminate it.

In all libraries the reasoning behind the rule and the state or local law references for each rule violation should be given for each policy and procedure. Note that although policies are public knowledge, most libraries—on the advice of law enforcement staff—do not share the enforcement procedures with the public "so individuals cannot 'game the system.'"

Policies and procedures in hand, some libraries are taking a harder stance on disruptive behavior, not just blatantly illegal activities. Disruptive behavior is commonly defined as an activity that interrupts the library's work, endangers anyone, or interferes with other patrons or staff. For example, it used to be that libraries did not ask patrons to leave the library unless they physically mistreated people or property. Now libraries are acting proactively, using progressive discipline and stiffer penalties with irate patrons who are out of control. The Alliance Library System (East Peoria, IL) publishes the *Safe Harbor Manual*, which includes a "Sample Policy on Angry or Irate Customers," which reads: "Excessive displays of anger directly to any employee or member of the public are not tolerated. If an employee feels uncomfortable or intimidated by the level of anger directed at them by a customer, he or she has both the right to insist the customer discontinue this behavior immediately, and a responsibility to defuse the situation."

The current "Rules of Conduct of the Seattle Public Library" state that it will "exclude any person who willfully and persistently violates these rules. . . . The rules will be enforced in a fair and reasonable manner with exclusion periods that vary based on the category of violation, with longer exclusion periods for Category A to Category E violations." Category A lists "Library Specific Behavior," such as engaging in disruptive behavior, leaving unattended packages, making inappropriate use of library property, and "failing to comply with a reasonable staff request to cease behavior that interferes with the effective functioning of the library." Category B lists "Serious Library Specific Violations," including "verbally or physically harassing other patrons, volunteers or staff, including stalking, staring or lurking." Category C consists of "Drug or Alcohol Possession or Use." Category D is "Violation Toward Person(s) or Property" and includes "intimidating staff, volunteers or other patrons" and "engaging in any other behavior that would constitute a misdemeanor under applicable law." Category E is "Serious Violation Toward Person(s) or Property," which includes "Verbally or physically threatening other patrons, volunteers and staff."

Currently in many libraries (if not most) a furious, screaming person who is frightening other patrons or staff may be asked to lower his or her voice. If the behavior persists, the person may be asked to leave until he or she calms down. If the person does not comply, he or she is "suspended" (asked to leave for a specified amount of time) or "excluded."

For example, the San Francisco (CA) Public Library's "Guidelines for Library Use" lists prohibited activities, including "Any activity that reasonably interferes with Library user or staff comfort, safety, use or quiet and peaceful enjoyment of the Library, including but not limited to harassing or threatening Library users or staff..." and three other activities. One of these is "Making any loud or unreasonable noise or other disturbance...." A screaming patron is breaking the rules, both by interfering with staff and user comfort and by being loud. The guidelines continue:

> Persons who violate these Guidelines may receive a warning from the Library staff and/or an opportunity to cease the violation or leave the Library. Illegal activity, as well as any willful or repeated violations of these Guidelines or other posted Library regulations (e.g., computer use rules) may result in removal from the Library and/or suspension of Library privileges. In addition, where authorized by Federal, State or local law, violations of these Guidelines may also result in arrest.

The Fresno (CA) Public Library recently revised its behavior policy and manual. A major change is that "authority to suspend patrons" for up to four weeks was given to all staff. All staffers are told: "[I]f you witness a rule violation, it is your responsibility to address the situation and fill out the form."

In all libraries, when a patron is suspended, he or she should be given the suspension in writing, usually a printed form including his or her name, library card number, specific dates of and reasons for suspension, signed and dated by the staff member. (If the disruptive behavior occurs while a patron is using a computer, a warning or two and the suspension notice can be sent directly to that computer screen.) Some libraries use a "notice of exclusion" or "notice of trespass" that requires the patron's signature and/or a physical description of the person. Sometimes the form distinguishes between prohibiting a person from entering the premises and prohibiting the use of library services; a patron may be suspended for one or both of these privileges. The suspension form should also explain how the patron can appeal the penalty and include a deadline for doing so.

Copies of the notice, in print or electronic form, should go to the supervisor, library director (or designee), head of security (if there is one), the library's counsel, and the police department. Copies should also be added to the Staff Incident Log, physical or electronic, and posted on the staff intranet (or bulletin board) so that everyone is aware of the suspension.

Stress Point Identification

Every library has certain policies, procedures, equipment, and so forth that consistently cause outbursts from patrons. Identifying these recurring irritants—or stress points—is essential if staff are to be well prepared to serve patrons.

Think about your library and what seems to aggravate your patrons. Record your thoughts in the Stress Points Exercise. Then, suggest to your supervisor that everyone in the department do the exercise on their own before discussing the questions as a group at a staff meeting.

EXERCISE

Stress Points

What causes patrons to be angry in your library? Check all that apply and add others based on your experiences.

___ Waiting in line

___ Circulation periods

___ Overdue fines

___ Reserve policies

___ Computers down

___ Insufficient Internet access stations

___ Insufficient express stations

___ Requirements for getting a library card

___ Lack of change for copiers

___ Books not on shelf as expected

___ Insufficient seating

___ Insufficient tables

___ Overcrowded programs

___ Behavior of other patrons

___ Noncirculating materials

___ No quiet room for contemplation or reading

___ No study rooms for small groups

___ Broken equipment

___ No eating or drinking allowed

___ Other—please explain:

Rebuttal Files

Commonly used by salespeople, a rebuttal file is a series of scripts for answering the most common complaints. Some libraries provide scripts for their staff, too. For example, the Dayton and Montgomery (OH) Public Library provides scripts in their *Customer Service Language Manual.* Although no one should simply read a script to an angry (or any) patron, writing possible responses out ahead of time can be good preparation.

Script preparation is best done as a group activity. All the staff in a department or unit should meet and brainstorm alternative answers to patrons who are upset by a specific stress point. These scripts are then presented in role plays so that all participants can see how they might play out. After more discussion on them, the responses are rewritten and retried until the staff members feel comfortable with the various possibilities for that stress point. And so on.

Scripting and practicing rebuttals not only increases staff's confidence in dealing with difficult situations but also assures that staff responses are reasonably consistent.

Quick Reference Guides

Quick reference guides—also called "cheat sheets" (see samples in Figure 8.1)—are kept at the service desks for staff to remind them of basic points to make or a rebuttal script to use if they become stuck during an exchange with an angry patron. Another quick reference guide should be posted to inform staff what to say if they need to call the police. Libraries should make their own cheat sheets based on their policies and procedures as well as the common stress points that staff have identified.

Figure 8.1. Sample Quick Reference Guides

With an Angry Patron	*With Unacceptable Behavior*	*When Calling Police*
• Breathe. • Don't take it personally. • Listen first. • Show sympathy for the situation. "It is frustrating to…" • Don't justify. • Don't argue. "That's a possibility." • It's okay for the patron to feel differently from you. "You may be right." • Watch your body language. • Talk to yourself: "I can handle this. This is not about me." • Offer options. "Here are some things we can do." • Call in a coworker to help you.	• Show good faith. • Label the behavior, not the person. • State your response to the behavior. • Suggest alternatives. • Be clear and assertive. • If the behavior persists, call security.	• Phone number of police: _____ • Identify yourself as staff of the library. • State your name and department. • Specify the level of the problem (e.g., any weapon, anyone hurt). • Describe where you and the patron are, including entrance closest to you. • Briefly describe the situation. • Describe the patron (height, weight, age, race, hair color). • Do not hang up until you receive instructions.

Incident Reports

The most important follow-up to any encounter with an angry patron is the incident report or log. Most libraries have incident report forms for use when police or security are called, or if anyone has been physically hurt or any property has been damaged, but similar forms should also be used for every event of anger or confrontation.

The form, whether hard copy or electronic, should include the date and time, the location (e.g., branch or department), the staff person's name, the patron's name and library card number (if known), a physical description of the patron, the presenting issue (e.g., upset that the library no longer keeps a record of all the materials he or she has checked out during the past year), and the resolution (e.g., suspension or not). It should allow enough space for the staff person to describe the incident. The form should be filled out by any and all staff members involved in the incident (not by a supervisor) and submitted to the supervisor with a copy to the director and to security (if the library has such). In a large library or system, these forms should be faxed or e-mailed to an administrator assigned to handle them so that immediate feedback can be given to all staff members involved and, when necessary, to other departments and branches so that they are alerted to situations as they develop. See Figure 8.2 for a sample form.

In some libraries this type of information is entered and kept as a computer record rather than in hard copy. This way, staffers can select from a standardized list of policy violations and problem behaviors. They can also access files to determine whether, for example, a patron has a legitimate issue or is a habitual complainer. For example, a patron who brings an overdue notice to the desk along with a book he claims to have found on the shelf may have caught a staff error (i.e., the book was shelved but not scanned in) or may be using a common tactic to avoid overdue fines. Although some libraries have determined that such files may leave the library open to lawsuits, the current trend is toward maintaining electronic incident logs.

Whether paper or electronic, incident forms are extremely useful for a number of reasons, including:

- Provide a chance to "get it off your chest" for the staff person involved; this is especially significant if there is no buddy system.
- Serve as a basis for future training; common scenarios can be used to train new or existing staff in defusing anger and handling complaints.
- Create a record of difficult patrons to alert other staff; if the same person habitually exhibits problem behaviors, a plan of action can be developed.
- Keep a record of trends in patron behavior.

Figure 8.2. Sample Incident Report Form

Date and time: _____

Location (i.e., branch or department): _____

Initial staff person: _____

Other staff involved: _____

Patron name (if known): _____

Patron's library card # (if known): _____

Patron description:

Issue (i.e., stress point):

Resolution:

Notes (e.g., what the library might do to affect this stress point; what the staff person might do differently next time; request for follow-up by staff member):

- Support consideration of policy or procedure changes; if certain policies or procedures often upset patrons, the library administration and board should be alerted.

- Provide information for the library board and/or city council; a composite portrait of the year's incidents can assist the powers that be to view the library (and its staffing needs) realistically.

- Document the need for security staff.

- Provide documentation for the police and/or court system should legal action become necessary.

- Ensure that supervisors have the information necessary to support and congratulate staff for their work.

Security and Other Staff

There are no national statistics on the use of security officers in libraries. However, it appears that security staff is more prevalent in academic and special libraries than in public libraries and that many more public libraries have security staff now than in the past. In 2008, the Ohio Library Council surveyed its members and found that 25 percent have security staff, in house or contractual.

Warren Graham, who calls himself the "Black Belt Librarian," represents the consensus of library security managers when he states that all "security staff...should be library employees rather than contractors—they will be better trained and more accountable, and understand that library security is totally unique." Even when security personnel are managed by another city department, there's concern that the officers will not be as effective as when they are library employees. For example, when the Los Angeles (CA) Public Library's security personnel became part of the city's General Services Department, the long-term head of library security was concerned that "the new officers will think of themselves as 'police' who enforce regulations, rather than library security officers who preserve a certain library atmosphere while protecting the right of library access to everyone." In Elmhurst, Illinois, a suburb of Chicago, the security monitors are city employees, part time in the library and part time in the police department (not sworn officers but parking control officers or administrative assistants in the detective division). The library director reports that "the good news for us is that when they call 911, they know everyone who responds—and they know all of the troublemakers in town. Most of the time, people who cause trouble at the library cause trouble other places in town."

Unfortunately, according to many librarians, security officers who are library employees are not necessarily more successful with angry patrons than those who are not. Although they may have a more library-oriented approach, they may not recognize when anger is brewing or deal with it as effectively as frontline information, reference, and circulation staff. When asked about this, one library administrator reported—and others agreed—that "security tends to come on a little more strongly than I like even at the beginning of an interaction. When this happens, it escalates the situation rather than defusing it." Another said,

> When a patron is angry, librarians and other staff handle it. We only call security when a patron breaks a library policy or if we feel our safety is in jeopardy. If a situation spirals out of control, we call security which is effective in getting people to leave the library, but usually at this point the situation is so extreme we can't expect them to calm someone down.

An informal survey in 2009 of reference librarians, circulation staff, managers, and other library workers in 30 states revealed that many libraries have outsourced security to private companies that provide guards and are charged with their supervision. This is the approach of the Chicago Public Library, for example, which contracts for security officers at the main library downtown and at its branches. The Oakland (CA) Public Library has library-employed security staff at the main location and contract guards at the branches. Even some suburban libraries have at least part-time contractual security staff now. For example, the director of a suburban Illinois library told me that they employ security guards each evening and weekend during the school year,

> mainly to keep kids from misbehaving—although lately, there have been some incidents with adults. With the economic downturn, we've seen more irate and stressed-out adults. People get mad for the most ridiculous of reasons. Things are so busy at the library that there is no way the reference staff can handle reference/readers' advisory and discipline issues.

In libraries with private security guards, it is still common for reference and circulation staff to deal with most angry encounters; the officers step in only if an interaction becomes violent. As a reference librarian at the University of Colorado told me, "Security is called only if we feel threatened or endangered by a belligerent patron, or if we are uncomfortable enforcing a rule with an angry patron whose behavior is loud and disruptive." Many libraries reported that contract guards are rarely taught how to defuse a situation and may even inadvertently escalate it. The branch supervisor in a rural library system told me, "It depends on the patron's character. If they don't respect a badge, the anger escalates when the guard steps in." It can also depend on the guard's character. As the head of circulation at a suburban public library commented, "Only about half of our security officers can calm angry patrons; it completely depends on the officer's temperament." According to a number of library directors, private security guards often have inadequate training, poor communication skills, and high turnover rates.

A few innovative libraries have agreements with the local police department or social service agencies to have their employees work in the library, assisting both library patrons and staff with difficult situations. These people are paid out of the library budget but are hired and supervised by their respective departments. Following are three such examples from California.

Police Assistants

The Mountain View (CA) Public Library has police assistants (PAs) working in the library under the supervision of the city's police department. PAs differ from police in that they are not sworn officers, they wear different uniforms, they do not carry weapons, and they cannot make arrests. PAs are charged with community policing and doing outreach for the police department.

The library and the police department jointly wrote the job description and recruited and interviewed applicants. The library PAs receive direct supervision from both sworn officers (who have badges and guns) and nonsworn personnel of the police department, which provided the initial training, badge, uniform, and walkie-talkie radio. The library budget covers the library PAs' salaries.

Each shift the PA checks voicemail and e-mail from the police department and from library administration. Then he or she reads recent incident reports, checks in with the desk staff, and patrols the library floors and the building's exterior. Walking through the library, the PA chats with patrons, enforces the behavior policy, and watches for customer problems. If the PA sees a problem he or she will intervene, helping the staff. The PA also fills out the incident forms required by the library and the police department, something library staff usually dislike doing. Every Saturday afternoon a police assistant reads stories to children. According to 2008–2009 statistics, the police assistants most often enforced behavior policies. They also intervened in Internet issues and handled customers who were abusive to other patrons or to staff. The library reported that the number of abusive customers was surprisingly small, partly because "the presence of someone in a police uniform causes most people to behave better."

Karen Burnett, Library Services Director of Mountain View (CA) Public Library, reports that the great majority of library staff members are satisfied with the PAs. They feel more personally secure in and around the library, and they appreciate that the PAs take on unpopular policing chores (e.g., completing incident reports, handling problems between patrons, making calls to police). The library reports a reduced number of incidents, reduced staff workload, and reduced staff stress since the PAs began working at the library. She states,

> this project has been a success for both the police department and the library: the shared training and supervision and shared expenses are great, but more important is that the PAs are proactive, and provide better security and safety for the library. The police department appreciates the opportunity for community presence, education, and involvement.

She notes that not all jurisdictions (e.g., cities and counties) have police assistant positions.

Police Sergeant as Chief of Security

The San Francisco (CA) Public Library has long had a city police officer as chief of security. This position is funded by the library, as are a number of other security positions, some of whom are stationed at the main library downtown while the others rotate among the neighborhood branches.

Security staff is rarely called for angry patrons, Sergeant Patrick Kwan reports, but when they are asked by staff to intervene the patron usually becomes reasonable—"the uniform itself has a quieting effect." That is one advantage of having a police officer stationed at the library; another is that he or she has a better understanding of the local laws and regulations and the ability to reach the police department directly and quickly when needed.

All library public service staff members are taught that if an angry customer is shouting or breaking a library rule, they should give a warning that the person must either stop the behavior or leave the library. If the patron refuses to leave, or if a city or county law is broken, library staff should call security (or the police department). In San Francisco and many other locales, refusing to leave the library after being so directed is considered trespassing, which is a misdemeanor. In that case, library personnel are trained that they (or a security guard) can make a citizen's arrest and then call the police. If police officers arrive and determine that they cannot arrest the patron after the fact, a library staffer will make a citizen's arrest. Note that in most places, public library rules are city ordinances and consequently are enforceable by citizen's arrest or by the police.

In many states and local jurisdictions when an angry patron is cited by the police, the law broken is most often "intentional interference with lawful business," which includes interfering with "the employees of a public agency open to the public, by obstructing or intimidating those attempting to carry on business, or those persons there to transact business with the public agency." Trespassing—"refusing or failing to leave a public building of a public agency when requested"—may follow when an encounter escalates. Other typical laws that libraries may invoke are loitering—"lingering without a lawful purpose for being on the property" or "not using the library as a library"—or "disorderly conduct." For more on laws and libraries, see the Policies and Procedures section in this chapter.

Social Worker in the Library

Since January 2009, the San Francisco (CA) Public Library has had a full-time psychiatric social worker stationed at Main. Leah Esguerra, MFT, is employed by the city Department of Public Health (DPH), Division of Behavioral Health (previously called Mental Health), and paid with library funds. She considers it advantageous to be a DPH employee because she has access to client records and has clinical support when she needs it.

She acts as a consultant to library staff about patrons with anger or mental health problems and gives staff feedback on how they handle confrontations. She also holds workshops for staff on how to set limits with patrons, which she considers "self-empowerment." The most common situations that lead library staff at Main to call her are needy individuals who demand an inordinate amount of staff time, potentially litigious people, and patrons who don't recognize limits. In the branches without full-time security officers, staffers most often discuss problem situations with substance abusers and angry people. According to Luis Herrera, the library's director, "an ongoing survey of staff and patrons shows fewer incidents of negative behaviors like yelling at others, and for those incidents that continue, a decrease in intensity."

The social worker's main responsibility is supervising the "health and safety associates" (HASAs). These are formerly homeless people who are paid to work with library patrons who are currently homeless. Modeled after a program at the Free Library of Philadelphia, and originally called bathroom monitors, HASAs make the bathrooms "safe and comfortable for patrons and staff" by patrolling through the public bathrooms. They also patrol the third, fourth, and fifth floors to see if people are sleeping, intoxicated, or causing trouble, and they distribute lists of shelters, drop-in centers, and other resources to anyone who appears to need help. The HASAs also serve as inspiration for homeless people. HASAs are hired as part of a vocational rehabilitation program when they are still DPH clients. Once they graduate from the program, they become employees of the homeless outreach team at DPH, working more hours and at a higher hourly wage.

Esguerra also assists people who are psychotic or delusional and those who have serious psychological problems. She walks through the library frequently looking for "hot spots" (potential incidents), and a HASA or library staff member can call her for help with troubled library users. She calls herself "a bridge to community resources," and in the past year she has directed at least 150 homeless people and others into social services.

A social worker on staff is never a substitute for security. Occasionally, Esguerra and a security officer are both called; in those instances they decide together which one of them has the best solution. For example, when a patron appears to be mentally ill and "dangerous to self or others," either a social worker or a police officer can call for the person's involuntary commitment to a psychiatric unit for a maximum of 72 hours.

QUICK REVIEW

Finding Help

- Policies and procedures go a long way in preventing patron anger and supporting library staff.
- Policies should be written in clear and explicit language, be available to the public in multiple languages and formats, and be posted in the library and on the library's webpage.
- Behavior policies must focus on specific behavior, be applied equally to all patrons, and allow for patron appeals.
- Procedures for enforcing behavior policies are essential.
- All staff should attend mandatory training on the governing policies and procedures.
- Security staff in libraries has become widespread.
- Other tools for library staff include rebuttal files, quick reference guides, and incident reports.

Bibliography

Aguilar, Leslie, and Linda Stokes. *Multicultural Customer Service: Providing Outstanding Service Across Cultures.* New York: McGraw Hill, 1996.

Alliance Library System. *Safe Harbor: Policies and Procedures for a Safe Library.* Alliance Library System, 2003. http://www.alliancelibrarysystem.com/safeharbor.

American Library Association, Reference and User Services Association (RUSA). "Guidelines for Behavioral Performance of Reference and Information Service Providers." American Library Association, 2004. http://www.ala.org/mgrps/divs/rusa/resources/guidelines/guidelines.cfm.

———. "Guidelines for Implementing and Maintaining Virtual Reference Services." American Library Association, 2010. http://www.ala.org/mgrps/divs/rusa/resources/guidelines/virtrefguidelines.cfm.

———. "Guidelines for the Development of Policies and Procedures Regarding User Behavior and Library Usage." American Library Association, 2005. http://www.ala.org/mgrps/divs/rusa/guidelines.cfm.

Arterburn, Tom R. "Librarians: Caretakers or Crimefighters?" *American Libraries* 27, no. 7 (August 1996): 32–34.

Axtell, Roger E. *Gestures: The Do's and Taboos of Body Language Around the World.* New York: Wiley, 1991.

Bach, George R., and Herbert Goldberg. *Creative Aggression.* New York: Avon, 1974.

Baron, Sara. "Problem or Challenge? Serving Library Customers That Technology Left Behind." In *Helping the Difficult Library Patron: New Approaches to Examining and Resolving a Long-Standing and Ongoing Problem*, edited by Kwasi Sarkodie-Mensah, 129–148. Binghamton, NY: The Haworth Press, 2002. Copublished simultaneously in *The Reference Librarian* 75/76 (2002): 129–148.

Beagle Research. "Improving Service Businesses with Appointment Scheduling." Beagle Research, August 2009. http://www.beagleresearch.com/2009Downloads/FINALWPTT073109.pdf.

Blackshaw, Pete. *Satisfied Customers Tell Three Friends: Angry Customers Tell 3,000.* New York: Doubleday, 2008.

Bolton, Robert. *People Skills: How to Assert Yourself, Listen to Others, and Resolve Conflict.* New York: Simon and Schuster, 1979.

Bramson, Robert M. *Coping with Difficult People...in Business and in Life*, 2nd ed. New York: Ballantine, 1988.

Bullard, Sharon W. "Gypsies, Tramps and Rage: Coping with Difficult Patrons." In *Helping the Difficult Library Patron: New Approaches to Examining and Resolving a Long-Standing and Ongoing Problem*, edited by Kwasi

Sarkodie-Mensah, 245–252. Binghamton, NY: The Haworth Press, 2002. Copublished simultaneously in *The Reference Librarian* 75/76 (2002): 245–252.

Burnett, Karen E. "Reaching Out Together: Mountain View's Library/Police Department Partnership." *Clarion* 6, no. 1 (April 2010): 21.

Camaratta, Maria A. "Library Service to People with Mental Challenges: Progress Since the Americans with Disabilities Act of 1990." *Public Libraries* 48, no. 3 (May/June 2009): 6–12.

Caputo, Jeanette S. *The Assertive Librarian*. Phoenix, AZ: Oryx Press, 1984.

Caraulia, Algene P., and Linda K. Steiger. *Nonviolent Crisis Intervention: Learning to Defuse Explosive Behavior*. Brookfield, WI: CPI, 1997.

Chapman, Greta, Marjorie Brekke, Karen Burd, David Catelli, and Jason Walker. "People, Not Problems: Solutions for Sharing Library Space with All Age Groups." *Public Libraries* 46, no. 5 (September/October 2007): 24–26.

Chelton, Mary K. "The 'Problem Patron' Libraries Created." In *Helping the Difficult Library Patron: New Approaches to Examining and Resolving a Long-Standing and Ongoing Problem*, edited by Kwasi Sarkodie-Mensah, 23–32. Binghamton, NY: The Haworth Press, 2002. Copublished simultaneously in *The Reference Librarian* 75/76 (2002): 23–32.

Comstock-Gay, Stuart. "Disruptive Behavior: Protecting People, Protecting Rights." *Wilson Library Bulletin* 69, no. 6 (February 1995): 23–25.

Conroy, Barbara, and Barbara Schindler Jones. *Improving Communication in the Library*. Phoenix, AZ: Oryx Press, 1986.

Datamonitor. "Global Consumer Trends: Convenience." Datamonitor, August 13, 2009. http://www.datamonitor.com.

Elgin, Suzette Haden. *The Gentle Art of Verbal Self-Defense at Work*. New York: Prentice-Hall, 2000.

Ellis, Albert. *Anger: How to Live with It and without It*, revised and updated edition. Secaucus, NJ: Citadel Press, 2003.

"Ethics and Venting about Library Patrons." *GenX Library Manager* (blog). January 21, 2009. http://luvgardenias.blogspot.com/2009_01_01_archive.html.

Fairfax County Public Library. *Problem Behavior Manual*, 3rd ed. Fairfax, VA: Fairfax County Public Library, forthcoming.

Fescemyer, Kathy. "Healing After Unpleasant Outbursts: Recovering from Incidents with Angry Library Users." In *Helping the Difficult Library Patron: New Approaches to Examining and Resolving a Long-Standing and Ongoing Problem*, edited by Kwasi Sarkodie-Mensah, 235–244. Binghamton, NY: The Haworth Press, 2002. Copublished simultaneously in *The Reference Librarian* 75/76 (2002): 235–244.

Folger, Joseph P., and Marshall S. Poole. *Working through Conflict: A Communication Perspective*. New York: Scott Foresman, 1984.

"For Indignation, Press 1." *Money Magazine* 35, no. 1 (January 2006): 26.

Gentry, W. Doyle. *Anger Management for Dummies*. Hoboken, NJ: Wiley, 2007.

Goldberg, Stephanie. "News Sites Reining in Nasty User Comments." Cable News Network, July 19, 2010. http://www.CNN.com/2010/TECH/web/07/19/commenting.on.news.sites/index.html.

Goldman, Lea. "Anger Management." *Forbes* 147, no. 9 (2004): 54.

Gordon, Thomas. *Leader Effectiveness Training*. New York: Wyden, 1977.

Graham, Warren. *Black Belt Librarians: Every Librarian's Real World Guide to a Safer Workplace*. Charlotte, NC: Main Street Rag/Pure Heart, 2006.

Hartley, J. "Cooling the Customer with HEAT." In *Best Practices in Customer Service*, edited by R. Zemke and J.A. Woods. Amherst, MA: HRD Press, 1998.

Hilyard, Nann Blaine. "Dealing with Problem Behavior in the Library." *Public Libraries* 46, no. 5 (September/October 2007): 21–33.

King, David Lee. "Be Nice to Customers—Even Online." *David Lee King* (blog). April 29, 2009. http://www.davidleeking.com/2009/04/29/be-nice-to-customers-even-online.

Leland, Karen, and Keith Bailey. *Customer Service for Dummies*, 1st ed. Foster City, CA: IDG, 1995.

Leland, Karen, and Keith Bailey. *Customer Service for Dummies*, 3rd ed. Hoboken, NJ: Wiley, 2006.

Lerner, Harriet Goldhor. *The Dance of Anger*. New York: Harper, 1985.

"Library Bill of Rights." *Library Journal* 115, no. 6 (April 1, 1990): 30.

Luhn, Rebecca R. *Managing Anger*. Los Altos, CA: Crisp Publications, 1992.

Luntz, Frank. *Words That Work: It's Not What You Say, It's What People Hear.* New York: Hyperion, 2007.

Lustberg, Arch. *Controlling the Confrontation.* VHS. Towson, MD: Library Video Network, 1989.

———. *Face It: Using Your Face to Sell Your Message.* VHS. Towson, MD: Library Video Network, 2002.

Mansfield, Heather. "How to Effectively Manage Hate and Anger on Social Media Sites." *Nonprofit Tech 2.0: A Social Media Guide for Nonprofits* (blog). March 21, 2010. http://nonprofitorgs.wordpress.com/2010/03/21.

Matthews, Anne J. *Communicate: A Librarian's Guide to Interpersonal Communications.* Chicago: American Library Association, 1983.

McNeil, Beth, and Denise J. Johnson. *Patron Behavior in Libraries: A Handbook of Positive Approaches to Negative Situations.* Chicago: American Library Association, 1996.

Miller, Dennis. "An Attitude of Caring." *The Reference Librarian* 60 (1998): 139–144.

Minow, Mary. "Writing a Library Behavior Code" (webcast). December 10, 2009. The Infopeople Project, California State Library.

Morgan, Rebecca L. *Calming Upset Customers: Staying Effective During Unpleasant Situations.* Los Altos, CA: Crisp Publications, 1989.

Munro, Kali. "Conflict in Cyberspace: How to Resolve Conflict Online." KaliMunro.com, 2002. http://www.kalimunro.com/article_conflict_online.html.

Navarro, Joe. *What Every Body Is Saying: An Ex-FBI Agent's Guide to Speed-Reading People.* New York: Collins, 2008.

Ohio Library Council. "Ohio Library Safety & Security Survey." Ohio Library Council, April 2008. http://www.olc.org/pdf/LibrarySafetySecuritySurveyResults.pdf.

Osa, Justina O. "The Difficult Patron Situation: Competency-Based Training to Empower Frontline Staff." In *Helping the Difficult Library Patron: New Approaches to Examining and Resolving a Long-Standing and Ongoing Problem,* edited by Kwasi Sarkodie-Mensah, 263–276. Binghamton, NY: The Haworth Press, 2002. Copublished simultaneously in *The Reference Librarian* 75/76 (2002): 263–276.

Owens, Sheryl. "Proactive Problem Patron Preparedness." *Library and Archival Security* 12, no. 2 (1994): 11–23.

Porter, Michael, and David Lee King. "Dealing with Comments on Your Website." *Public Libraries* 48, no. 6 (November/December 2009): 23–25.

Radford, Marie L. "Investigating Interpersonal Communication in Chat Reference: Dealing with Impatient Users and Rude Encounters." In *The Virtual

Reference Desk: Creating a Reference Future, edited by R. David Lankes et al., 23–46. New York: Neal-Schuman, 2006.

Radford, Marie L., and Lynn Silipigni Connaway. "Getting Better All the Time: Improving Communication and Accuracy in Virtual Reference." In *Reference Renaissance: Current and Future Trends*, edited by Marie Radford and R. David Lankes, 39–54. New York: Neal-Schuman, 2010.

Rogers, Carl. *On Becoming a Person.* Boston: Houghton Mifflin, 1961.

Ross, Catherine Sheldrick, and Patricia Dewdney. *Communicating Professionally: A How-To-Do-It Manual for Library Applications*, 2nd ed. New York: Neal-Schuman, 1999.

Ross, Catherine Sheldrick, Kirsti Nilsen, and Marie L. Radford. *Conducting the Reference Interview: A How-To-Do-It Manual for Librarians*, 2nd ed. New York: Neal-Schuman, 2009.

Rubin, Rhea Joyce. "Anger at the Reference Desk (and Elsewhere)." In *The Reference Library User*, edited by Bill Katz, 34–52. Binghamton, NY: The Haworth Press, 1990.

———. "Defusing the Angry Patron." *Library Mosaics* 11, no. 3 (May/June 2000): 14–15.

Salter, Charles A., and Jeffrey L. Salter. *On the Frontlines: Coping with the Library's Problem Patrons.* New York: Libraries Unlimited, 1988.

Sarkodie-Mensah, Kwasi, ed. *Helping the Difficult Library Patron: New Approaches to Examining and Resolving a Long-Standing and Ongoing Problem.* Binghamton, NY: The Haworth Press, 2002. Copublished simultaneously as The Reference Librarian 75/76 (2002).

Shellenbarger, Sue. "The Domino Effect: The Unintended Result of Telling Off Customer Service Staff." *Wall Street Journal*, February 5, 2004, sec. D.

Shuman, Bruce. *Case Studies in Library Security.* New York: Libraries Unlimited, 2002.

———. "Designing Personal Safety into Library Buildings." *American Libraries* 27, no. 7 (August 1996): 37–39.

———. "Problem Patrons: Reviewing Your Options," *Public Libraries* 41, no. 6 (November/December 2002): 338–342.

———. *River Bend Revisited: The Problem Patron in the Library.* Phoenix, AZ: Oryx Press, 1984.

Slavick, Steven. "Problem Situations, Not Problem Patrons." *Public Libraries* 48, no. 6 (November/December 2009): 38–42.

Smith, Catherine. *Serving the Difficult Customer.* New York: Neal-Schuman, 1993.

Smith, Nathan M. "Active Listening: Alienating Patron Problems through Communication." In *Patron Behavior in Libraries: A Handbook of Positive Approaches to Negative Situations*, edited by Beth McNeil and Denise J. Johnson, 127–134. Chicago: American Library Association, 1996.

Smith, Nathan M., and Irene Adams. "Using Active Listening to Deal with Patron Problems." *Public Libraries* 30, no. 4 (July/August 1991): 236–239.

Spielberger, Charles, and Jerry Deffenbacher. "Strategies for Controlling Your Anger." American Psychological Association, n.d. http://www.apa.org/help center/controlling-anger.aspx.

Stone, Douglas, Bruce Patton, and Sheila Heen. *Difficult Conversations: How to Discuss What Matters Most.* New York: Viking Penguin, 1999.

Suler, John. "The Online Disinhibition Effect." Rider University, 2002. http://www.rider.edu/users/suler/psycyber/disinhibit.html.

Tannen, Deborah. "Apologies Make the World Go Round." *Civilization* 6, no. 2 (April/May 1999): 63.

——. *The Argument Culture: Stopping America's War of Words.* New York: Ballantine, 1999.

Tavris, Carol. "Anger Defused." *Psychology Today* 16, no. 11 (November 1982): 25–34.

——. *Anger: The Misunderstood Emotion.* New York: Simon and Schuster, 1982.

Thom, Nathaniel. Quoted in "Can Exercise Moderate Anger?" by Gretchen Reynolds. *New York Times Magazine*, August 15, 2010: 21.

Thompson, George J., and Jerry B. Jenkins. *Verbal Judo: The Gentle Art of Persuasion*, 2nd ed. New York: HarperCollins, 2004.

Torrey, E. Fuller, Rosanna Esposito, and Jeffrey Geller. "Problems Associated with Mentally Ill Individuals in Public Libraries," *Public Libraries* 48, no. 2 (March/April 2009): 45–51.

Turman, Janet. "Managing Difficult Situations in Public Library Service: A Continuing Process." Presentation at workshops in California, 1998.

——. "Managing Difficult Situations in Public Library Service: Procedures and Communication Skills for Supervisors." Presentation at the Annual Conference of the California Library Association, 1998.

Turner, Anne M. *It Comes with the Territory: Handling Problem Situations in Libraries.* Jefferson, NC: McFarland, 1993.

Turner, Diane J., and Marilyn Grotzky. "Help Yourself: Front-Line Defense in an Academic Library." In *Helping the Difficult Library Patron: New Approaches to Examining and Resolving a Long-Standing and Ongoing Problem*, edited by Kwasi Sarkodie-Mensah, 253–262. Binghamton, NY: The Haworth Press, 2002. Copublished simultaneously in *The Reference Librarian* 75/76 (2002): 253–262.

Waller, Elizabeth, and Patricia Bangs. "Embracing the Problem Customer." *Public Libraries* 46, no. 5 (September/October 2007): 27–28.

Walters, Suzanne. *Customer Service: A How-To-Do-It Manual.* New York: Neal-Schuman, 1994.

Weingand, Darlene. *Customer Service Excellence.* Chicago: American Library Association Editions, 1997.

Weisinger, Hendrie. *Dr. Weisinger's Anger Workout Book.* New York: Quill, 1985.

Wells, T. *Keeping Your Cool Under Fire.* New York: McGraw-Hill, 1980.

Weyant, Bob. *Confrontation without Guilt or Conflict.* Bellevue, WA: Brassy, 1994.

Willis, Mark R. *Dealing with Difficult People in the Library.* Chicago: American Library Association, 1999.

Index

Page numbers followed by the letter "f" indicate figures.

About the Author

Rhea Joyce Rubin has been an independent library consultant since 1980. She specializes in extending public library services to people who do not traditionally use the library, and in outcome measurement. Working exclusively with libraries, Rubin divides her time between consulting (problem solving, planning, and evaluation) and training. She has trained more than 10,000 librarians and paraprofessionals in more than 40 states.

She is the recipient of four awards from the American Library Association, including the Shaw Award for Library Literature in 1980 for her first two books. This revised edition of *Defusing the Angry Patron* is her thirteenth book.

For more about Rubin, see her profile in *Who's Who in the World, Who's Who of American Women, Who's Who in American Education*, or *Contemporary Authors*, or visit her website: http://www.rheajoycerubin.org.

CPSIA information can be obtained
at www.ICGtesting.com
Printed in the USA
FFOW05n1952080216